A TRUE HEART

THE FIGHTS OF MY LIFE

BILLY DIB

Copyright © Billy Dib
First published in Australia in 2023
by KMD Books
Waikiki, WA 6169

All rights reserved. No part of this book may be used or reproduced by any means, graphic, electronic, or mechanical, including photocopying, recording, taping or by any information storage retrieval system without the written permission of the copyright owner except in the case of brief quotations embodied in critical articles and reviews.

Because of the dynamic nature of the Internet, any web addresses or links contained in this book may have changed since publication and may no longer be vaild. The views expressed in this work are solely those of the author and do not necessarily reflect the views of the publisher and the publisher hereby disclaims any responsibility for them.

 A catalogue record for this work is available from the National Library of Australia

National Library of Australia Catalogue-in-Publication data:
A True Heart/Billy Dib

ISBN:
978-0-6457250-5-6
(Paperback)

ISBN:
978-0-6457250-8-7
(Hardback)

CONTENTS

FOREWORD..V
AN ODE TO EMAID VIII
PROLOGUE...1
EARLY DAYS..7
BOXING 11
PROFESSIONAL BOXING DEBUT..17
GOLDEN BOY...22
COMING HOME 29
MY FIRST DEFEAT..34
THE REBUILD 39
CHARGE TO THE WORLD TITLE 44
A LIFE-CHANGING MOMENT 52
FIRST WORLD TITLE DEFENCE..58
NEXT STEPS 63

COLLISION COURSE	69
SMS PROMOTIONS JOURNEY	80
GRADOVICH	84
THE REMATCH	91
NEXT STEPS	99
SARA	118
MY MOTHER	123
MOVING FORWARD	142
FIGHT DAY	151
MEETING MY FUTURE WIFE	165
SHOWDOWN	172
A WELCOME BACK	179
BERRY ONCE AGAIN FALLS PREGNANT	185
THE FARM	198
LAST FIGHT	206
MY JOURNEY THROUGH CANCER	215
THE ROLLER-COASTER CALLED CANCER	227
MONIQUE MAYERS	230
MRS CHETTY	232

FOREWORD

Life is never predictable; the mountainous highs and the valley lows all meld together to shape experience. We try as hard as possible to shape our lives the way we want, but it doesn't always work out the way we planned – there's always events we simply cannot control.

Our character, though, is something we have complete discretion over, and it's the way we respond to things beyond our control that demonstrates the true nature of a fire that burns within each and every one of us; that knowing of our limits, gritting our teeth, facing any challenge and never giving up.

Billy is my brother, I've been beside him from the moment he was an annoying kid, through to the world championships, into the nights of grieving silence and the fearful days listening to the constant beeps of medical machinery when his own mortality weighed heavily on our minds. As brothers, we have celebrated every success, cried over every setback and ridden every single wave of emotion through this extraordinary life of his.

I always knew Billy was going to be something special, he had a restless desire to be the best, and I remember him sharing his bright-eyed dream of becoming a world boxing champion. As all family would, I was supportive, but truth is, I never really thought he would achieve what he did, I expected it to be just another passing phase of a young idealist. His determination proved me and many others wrong; what I had underestimated was a person with the steeliest of wills. A young man who would pursue his dream with every fibre of his being.

The book details every element of the boxing journey in detail. Billy reflects on the emotions, the challenges, the training and the whole 'show' of the industry. He shares the exhilaration of victory and juxtaposes it with the devastation of losing. The funny stories, the let-downs and the travels of a brilliant career. Amongst all that, he shares the raw authenticity of everything happening around him, a magnificent insight into a world we don't see from outside the ring.

But there's so much more to my brother than boxing. There's the Billy that no-one really knows about; the visiting young people in jail to help change mindsets, there's the Billy that does a massive amount of charity work without anyone knowing, there's the Billy who takes in people who have nowhere else to turn, the Billy who feeds the homeless and there's the Billy who has always remained steadfast, true to his faith and humble beyond measure.

Most importantly, though, there's the Billy I most love: the mature man completely dedicated to his immediate and extended family. The Billy who, through all the adversity he has ever faced, has lived by the adage that no matter how many times you get knocked down in life, you have to get up one more time. Billy doesn't hold back on the devastating personal experiences he has had nor the mistakes he has made. This is a raw and authentic account of a life lived in the public domain.

This book gives an insight into an extraordinary human being, a man who has taken more in life than what could be seen as a fair share but still smiles through it. A man who, when the unexpected calamity happens, looks to find ways out of it rather than dwell on the misfortune. A man who inspires others through his journey of cancer and yet still finds a way to laugh and remain optimistic.

Yes – this is my brother and I may come with a bias but I'm so incredibly proud of him. He brings the best out in me and has taught me that every challenge is just another test. You'll always be the people's champion, Billy, and hopefully you keep inspiring others, as you do, me.

GRATITUDE
AN ODE TO EMAID

One of the major conductors of my career, my brother Emaid, has had my back since day one. A successful car salesman who went on to become Australia's leading BMW sales manager, Emaid took control of my flourishing boxing career from a very early age. He was there as a major support for much of my amateur career and I can recall him taking me under his wing and dropping me to fights all over Sydney. He was there with me to celebrate my triumphs and was there to uplift me when I took my losses.

Emaid's business sense and negotiation skills developed in his personal career helped him become a top-shelf boxing manager, and I credit him with a lot of my success. He was able to provide me with many big fight opportunities and I entrusted him with sealing deals with the various promoters that I dealt with in my career. He endured many sleepless nights, spent endless hours on the phone to overseas contacts in order to give me the best shot at fulfilling my dream, just a part of the reason that I will be forever grateful.

Together, we made sure that the boxing world took notice. Together, we conquered the boxing world and reached the absolute pinnacle of the sport. Emaid Dib. My right hand man!

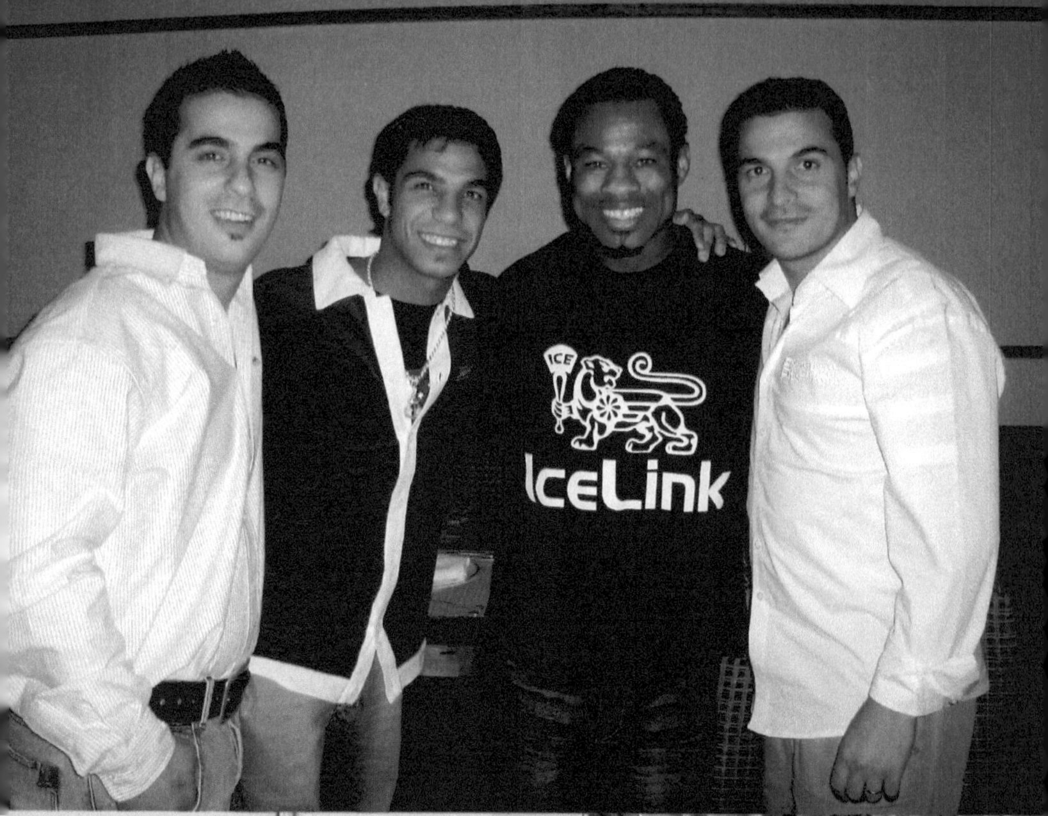
ICE
IceLink

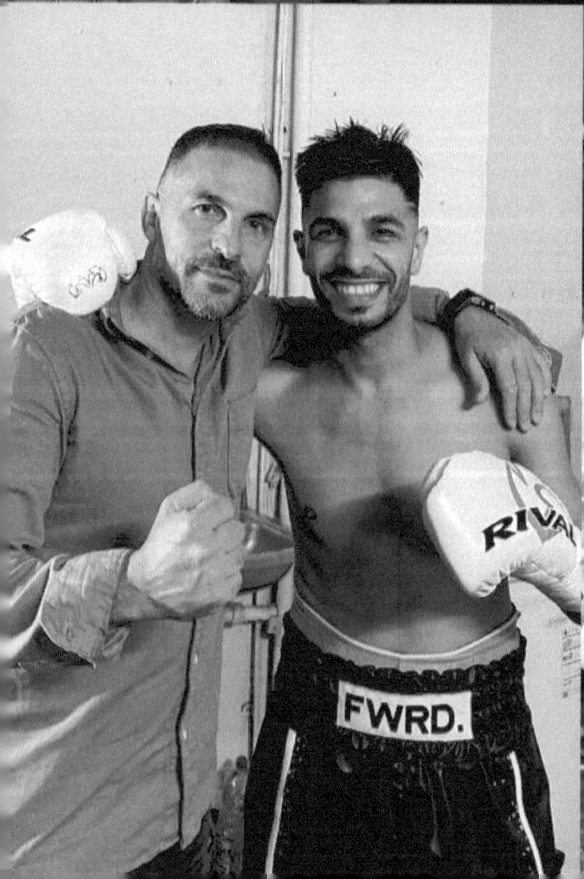
RIVAL
FWRD.

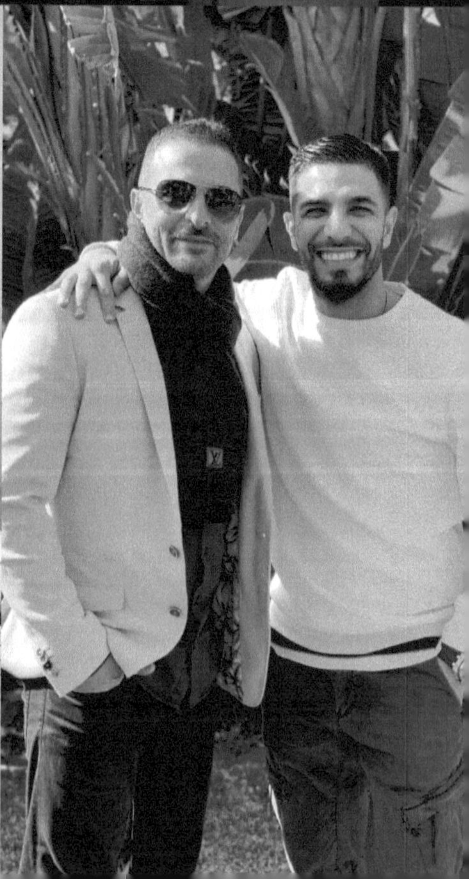

PROLOGUE

The punch to the guts that sent me to the floor of the hospital room hit me far harder than any KO I've ever experienced. As I open my eyes and adjust to the dim light, I reach for Sara's hand, and try to lift myself from the floor to gaze on her pale, serene face for what could be the last time.

'I want to tell you everything, Sara, and I know you can hear me. The machines keeping you alive tell a different story; the doctors have told me your time is short. We've only been together as a couple for eighteen months and I feel there's so much more I want to tell you.'

I can see the ref standing over me, counting down my time, and maybe it's just enough to share some of my life memories and stand-out moments with you …

ONE

I was destined to be a fighter from the day I was born, suffering chronic asthma for the first few months of my life. And that fight for survival continued as we were one of only two Lebanese families growing up in a suburb of Sydney. I was bullied constantly, and I still remember the fear of going to school every single day. But in hindsight, that experience taught me to fight with resilience, persistence and humility.

TWO

Dad insisted I play rugby to try to 'fit in', and it was my rugby coach who suggested I try boxing after a pad-work session. 'Have you ever boxed before?' he asked in surprise.

'No,' I replied. 'All I know about boxing is from watching the Sylvester Stallone *Rocky* movies.' My destiny was paved from the moment I walked into the boxing gym at Sutherland PCYC.

THREE

I was blessed with an impressive amateur career, representing Australia in every possible competition (except for one) and joining the Australian Institute of Sport in Canberra to prepare for the pinnacle of amateur boxing: the Olympic Games. I was well prepared to represent Australia at the 2004 Olympics in Greece, but a quirk of fate would put an end to that! Why oh why did I believe I could ride my brother's powerful R6 Yamaha motorbike having only just passed my test? I was lucky I was wearing a helmet. Not so lucky that I was wearing only a singlet, shorts and sneakers, burning the skin off my arms, legs and shoulders, which took some time to heal. No Olympic Games for me!

FOUR

A lot happened in 2004. After missing out on the Olympic Games, I was blessed to have the opportunity to meet my childhood boxing hero, Prince Naseem Hamed after travelling to meet him in London at his request. I broke down in tears as he opened the door, it was so overwhelming. He convinced me to become a 'professional' fighter and I laced up my gloves for my first professional bout just three days before my nineteenth birthday. Four months and three winning bouts later, I gained my first professional title of Australian Super Featherweight.

FIVE

My first international bout came just a few months later in the UK, and although things didn't go exactly to plan, I went on to win and was then at 10-0 in just fifteen months in my professional boxing career. Unfortunately, my personal life wasn't great and my fiancée, of four years, and I split just days before my twenty-first birthday. My brother organised a special dinner to cheer me up, and legendary Jeff Fenech attended. 'I'm taking you with me to Las Vegas,' he said, 'and we're going to train with Mike Tyson!'

SIX

At just twenty-one years old, the trip to Las Vegas was amazing. Not only did I have the chance to train alongside one of the sport's greatest stars of the previous two decades, but it also saw me sign with one of the biggest promotional companies in the world: Golden Boy Promotions. It gave me the opportunity to hang out with some of the greats in boxing and fight on top cards in the US at some of the best-known stadiums including Madison Square Garden. I attended training camps with legendary boxers and was blessed to be a part of the night on one of boxing's highest grossing fights of all time – the fight between Oscar De La Hoya and Floyd Mayweather, the headline event. At this point, I was 16-0 and well on my way in my journey toward becoming a world champion.

SEVEN

After two years without a bout in Australia, and a record of 20-0 in my professional career, I was excited to be able to challenge for the IBO Super Featherweight World Title on home soil, in Newcastle, NSW, against Zolani Marali. I put a lot of pressure on myself prior to the fight, and it was a brutal twelve rounds before I secured victory to become world champion for the first time. A week or so later, we were informed that Marali's team had lodged a protest and a rematch would need to be fought. Golden Boy Promotions told me we had bigger fish to fry and to vacate the title. They came good on their promise, delivering me a title shot against the reigning WBO Featherweight World Champion, Steve Luevano. This would give me the opportunity to win a second world title in another division, although it came at short notice. Long story very short ... I was 1.1kg over the required weight of 57.2kg on the day of the weigh-in. I only just made weight, severely dehydrated. I suffered my first ever professional defeat in that bout, in what was described as lacklustre and boring. I was devastated.

EIGHT

After being blessed with an invitation to the Islamic Pilgrimage to the holy city of Mecca, referred to as 'Hajj', and the trip to Saudi Arabia, which literally changed my life, it wasn't long before I was back training with a new trainer, Billy Hussein. I never imagined I'd be lucky enough to be training with Billy, and he insisted we get through ten fights before I go for any championship-level fight. It was Billy who was able to turn me into a well-rounded fighter instead of just a 'slick boxer'. In July 2011, I defeated Jorge Lacierva to become the IBF Featherweight Champion. My reign as featherweight world champion, from 2011-2013, were some of the best years of my life.

NINE

In July 2012, I met with 50 Cent, half of exciting new boxing promotion company, TMT Promotions, along with Floyd Mayweather. After an amazing night in Las Vegas, I signed with TMT for a three-year, nine-fight deal worth over $2 million. It was an exciting time, but short-lived as just four months later, TMT Promotions fell apart. I ended up signing with SMS Promotions, solely owned by 50 Cent, but I got caught up in the crossfire of the TMT breakup, not fighting for over seven months for a variety of reasons. It was in March 2013 that I lost my IBF title in a fight against Evgeny Gradovich that left me battered and bruised, but we scheduled our rematch in Macao for November of the same year. His punches seemed so much more powerful the second time around, I wondered if his gloves were loaded! We were on an even par until the sixth round when I suffered a blow to the canvas – only the third in my career. From there, things didn't go well, and it was my trainer, Billy Hussein, who stopped the fight in the ninth round.

TEN

The months following my defeat were difficult, with me doubting so much about myself and where I was in my life. But that's when I met you, Sara. You turned my life around. Even my thoughts around boxing became positive again, as Billy Hussein had confirmed my next fight would be in July 2014. One of my happiest-ever days was 27 April of that year, when we performed our Fatihaa, confirming our intention to spend the rest of our lives together, in front of our family and friends.

I'll never forget those wonderful thirteen months we spent getting to know each other prior to our engagement on 31 August 2015. I knew I had found my soulmate in you and life seemed perfect. I had even worked my way back into the world rankings with some convincing wins over talented opponents. Your support during my unsuccessful challenge for the WBC Super-Featherweight Title was what got me through my defeat by a third-round TKO.

But that knockout is nothing compared to the punch of learning you had cancer, and now, lying on the hospital floor, watching you in your last hours. I hear the count and lift myself to rest my head on your chest. I know it's time to say goodbye. I will love you forever, and with your inspiration and blessing, I won't let your passing define me. I will miss you and mourn you, but I will continue to keep fighting and to look for the joy in life. Life is precious, and you have taught me it can change in the blink of an eye, and so, in your honour, I will try to be present and live life to the fullest … whatever that may be.

And the story continues …

CHAPTER ONE
EARLY DAYS

I was born Bilal Mohammed Ali Dib on 17 August 1985, at St George Hospital, Sydney, and I was destined to be a fighter that very same day. The first few months of my life were spent in and out of hospital as I battled with chronic asthma. Upon leaving the hospital as a newborn, a man, described by my mother as old, grey and pious, approached my parents. He took one look at me and said, 'Someday, this boy will be well-known and will impact many lives.' My mother didn't tell me about this moment until much later in my life.

I attended Engadine Public School from the age of five, and to say it was a constant struggle would be an understatement. Every day was a daunting experience, waking each morning, wondering what another day of school had in store for me. I honestly can't count the amount of fights I had – because of racism.

As one of only two Lebanese families in Engadine, growing up was really tough. I never felt accepted and it seemed every day there would be an altercation involving my older brothers or me.

My father decided to sign me up with the local rugby league team, the Bosco Bulldogs, in the hope that participating in a team sport would help me connect with the other kids at school. 'Kill them with kindness,' my dad would say. Whilst I wasn't much of a rugby league fan, at just twelve years old, it was there on the football field I would meet my destiny.

As a young boy, my first recognisable hero was none other than Rocky Balboa. One night at footy training, the coach pulled out a bag full of boxing gloves and pads, and somewhat instinctively, I picked up a set of mitts and started to let my hands fly. From the moment my gloves first pounded against the pads, I had found my true calling. My coach must have seen it too, as he stopped me, grabbed a set of pads and asked me to throw a few different combinations.

He asked if I had ever boxed, to which I replied, 'No, but I've watched all the *Rocky* movies.' He suggested I should get my father to take me to local Sutherland PCYC to try the sport of boxing.

Convincing my father to do that seemed a steep mountain to climb, as I was already quite an aggressive kid having grown up with six siblings, five of them boys. Fighting was a regular occurrence in our household, along with all the fighting that went on at school. Meanwhile, rugby league was extremely popular amongst our extended family, my father being a massive fan of Mal Meninga, one of the best ever to grace the rugby league field. I was pretty sure he wanted one of his sons to emulate his favourite athlete. 'Dad,' I prompted, 'I was speaking to my footy coach, and he suggested you take me to the PCYC to take up some boxing.' His eyebrows raised and I quickly added, 'It will help me with my cardio and he thinks it'd make me a better rugby league player.'

Whilst I could tell he wasn't convinced, he agreed.

CHAPTER TWO
BOXING

I walked up the stairs at the Sutherland PCYC into the boxing gym, my heart pounding, unsure of what to expect. I was anxious, but also so excited; I already had my gloves on, wedging a one-dollar coin between the thumbs of my glove to pay for the session. I opened the gym door and was immediately greeted by a man by the name of Rusty. 'Why have you got your gloves on?' he asked.

'I'm here to fight!' I exclaimed.

My destiny was paved from the very moment I stepped into that boxing gym. It was right then I decided boxing was what I wanted to do. I became super-obsessed with the sport – very quickly. I rented every boxing documentary I could find, and *Fenech Fighter*, a documentary on Australia's own boxing legend, Jeff Fenech, became my favourite. After just a month or so at the gym, I convinced my trainer,

Rusty, to put me into an exhibition match with experienced amateur, Tommy Browne.

Six months on, my cousin, Gary Ghasser, who has always supported me, introduced me to a man who would change the whole trajectory of my life and go on to become somewhat of a second father to me. That man was Haidar 'Harry' Hammoud. Harry came to meet me at my home in Engadine. He asked me how many fights I'd competed in and to throw a few punches. I wanted to impress him so told him I'd already had thirteen amateur bouts, even though I only had one exhibition bout to my name.

It wasn't until my first real fight that I eventually told Harry I hadn't actually had any fights. I lost my first fight to Shane Georges, a kid who would go on to become an amateur rival of mine. The fight took place at Bankstown PCYC and felt like a blur at the time. His trainer was well-renowned amateur boxing coach, Billy Hussein. It's funny the way the world works. The trainer who was in the opposite corner to me would go on to play a major role in both my amateur and professional boxing career.

Despite picking up a loss in my first fight, I went on to have an outstanding amateur career, consisting of 113 bouts for 98 wins, competing and representing Australia in almost every single major amateur tournament there was. A few of the amateur fights I had which stood out to me were fights against the likes of Daniel O'Hara, Tommy Browne, Greg Eadie and Ryan Langham, each of whom were great amateur boxers in their own right. A few of the biggest tournaments I competed in during my amateur career were the World Cadet Championships in Hungary, World Junior Championships in Cuba and the World Championships in Thailand. It was a dream of mine to be able to represent Australia at the Olympic Games, the absolute pinnacle of amateur boxing. And it was all Harry and I would talk about from

1999 onwards.

At the age of thirteen, Harry gave me a video cassette titled, *Licence to Thrill*. It became my most-watched video as I was immersed in the boxing style of the amazing featherweight world champion, Prince Naseem Hamed. With my eyes glued to the television, the ultra-talented and flamboyant Hamed immediately became my childhood hero and I had decided who I wanted to emulate in my boxing career. Dreaming I would someday meet him, I wrote to his fan page over three hundred times.

As I continued to pursue my boxing career, racking up a number of important wins along the way and joining the Australian Institute of Sport (AIS) in Canberra, my vision was most firmly set on reaching the 2004 Olympic Games in Athens, Greece. However, an ill-fated decision to leave the AIS and complete the final couple of weeks preparation for the Olympic Games trials in my hometown of Sydney ultimately put a stop to my dream coming to fruition.

During my time in Sydney, I decided to get a motorcycle license. Just a few weeks out from the Olympic trials, my older brother, Mouhammad, came home on an R6 Yamaha motorbike. He asked me to wash it and I was told not to ride it – under *any* circumstances. Mouhammad went off to run a few errands, and for some reason, I had a brain snap; I decided I would take the bike for 'a *quick* ride'. The bike was powerful, and I couldn't control it. I fell off, sliding down 20m of road wearing only a singlet, shorts and sneakers, burning the skin off my arms, legs and shoulders. It was lucky I had at least put on a helmet.

It took some time for me to recover from the burns, hindering my preparation for the trials. I watched as my dreams crumbled. The eventual winner of the Australian Olympic trials, Ryan Langham, I had previously stopped in an earlier box-off to represent Australia in my 57kg weight category.

It was painful enough dealing with the burns from the motorbike accident but dealing with the emotional torment and missing out on my Olympic dream was far worse. I was left feeling empty and lost. This was something I had worked so hard for and a stupid decision to get on my brother's bike had left me paying a hefty price. I was reeling. I didn't feel like getting out of bed for several weeks.

A few weeks passed and I met someone who was to become a prominent figure in my life. That man was Adam Houda. At a gathering with some mutual friends, Adam and I had a conversation which ultimately led to me leaving the amateur boxing circuit for the professional boxing ranks. Adam and I talked all things boxing, and upon my mentioning of Prince Naseem Hamed, Adam told me he knew of someone who might be able to arrange a meeting between me and Hamed. After a few days, my younger sister came home with a pamphlet advertising that Prince Naseem Hamed would be attending Lakemba Mosque as a guest speaker. I couldn't hide my excitement. I reached the mosque an hour before the event was scheduled to begin and sat in anticipation, while Sheikh Khalid Yasin, a prominent Islamic leader from America, took to the podium to give a talk. He explained that Hamed would be joining us as a guest speaker via video link from the UK. I was devastated, realising I wouldn't have the opportunity to meet my hero after all. When the talk concluded, I approached Sheikh Yasin and begged him to call Hamed back and let me talk to him. Fifteen minutes on, he presented me with an offer. He told me about One Islam Productions and organised a meeting between me and the man who ran the company. It was Subhi who helped me to put together a biography and video with highlights of my amateur career. I later gave the video to Sheikh Yasin and he promised he would have Prince Naseem call me. I was excited but knew there was a chance it may not happen.

About a week later, I received a phone call from a strange number.

'Hello, is that Bilal?' I was in instant shock. I couldn't believe what was happening. 'It's the Prince, Habibi.' My hero, a man who I'd tried to get in contact with for almost five years, was calling me. I ran around the house telling everyone Naseem Hamed was on the phone. We had an in-depth, thirty-minute chat, cultivating in Naz asking me when I would go to the UK to visit him.

It was only a few days before I found myself on a plane, UK bound. On the way, I could barely sleep knowing I was on the way to meet my childhood hero. On arrival at the airport, a man was holding a sign with my name on it and told me he would take me to Sheikh Yasin's home. Days passed and Naz still hadn't shown. By then, I had started to get nervous, doubting our meeting would happen. Three days after my arrival, I asked Sheikh Yasin if he would take me to a boxing gym so I could get some training in. To my surprise, I found myself at a gym where I trained alongside the likes of UK legend Kell Brook, and even sparred a few rounds with the former IBO Cruiserweight Champion, Johnny Nelson. As I was wrapping up my session, a driver walked in and told me he would be taking me to meet Naz.

After a ten-minute drive, we arrived at a home which resembled the White House. I hit the doorbell nervously. There he was, the one and only, Prince Naseem Hamed. I instantly broke down into tears, knowing how long I had waited for that moment. As the days and weeks passed, I tried to soak in as much knowledge as I could. As my time in the UK came to an end, Naz convinced me I would be better suited to the professional ranks, promising to guide both my trainer, Harry, and me throughout my professional career.

CHAPTER THREE
PROFESSIONAL BOXING DEBUT

It was 15 August 2004, just three days short of my nineteenth birthday, that I would lace up my gloves as a professional for the very first time, dominating my opponent, Chad Roy Naidu, en-route to a fourth-round stoppage. I had announced myself as a prospect to watch out for. Four months on and three fights later, I would find myself competing for the Australian Super Featherweight title against Jungstar Min, stopping him in the second round and capturing my first professional title in the process. Looking back, I realise this was a great achievement, but at the time, I was so focused on moving forward to my next fight and working towards becoming a world champion.

I was soon back on a plane headed for the UK to live and train alongside Prince Naseem for what became a very memorable three weeks. Naz took me under his wing, spending time with me not only in the gym, but outside of it too. We became somewhat like brothers, as he told everyone who would listen that I was a 'future world champion'. There were many times I felt I needed to pinch myself, to make sure it wasn't all a dream. It was unreal and humbling, as Naz would spend hours dissecting footage from my fights, critiquing me on what I needed to do better to improve my game. Each time I left the UK, I felt I was leaving a more complete fighter and human being, gaining confidence that I would reach my ultimate goal of becoming a world champion.

More wins were piling up back home, as I amassed a record nine victories and no defeats. Nearly a year after my previous visit to the UK, Naz secured me a spot on Ricky Hatton's undercard – my first international bout. I was slated to face the experienced Buster Dennis in a six-round contest. Having trained for almost five weeks in the UK, I was devastated to learn my opponent didn't turn up to the weigh-in. The promoter scrambled to find a replacement opponent, with Imad Khamis stepping up to the plate. My team had some deliberating to do, however, as Khamis weighed in 5.5kg heavier than me. I did not want to let the preparation I had go to waste and pleaded with my team to let the fight go ahead, promising to take a safety-first approach. I did that, cruising to a six-round decision victory, taking every round on the scorecards.

I was undefeated as a professional, amassing a record of 10-0 in just fifteen months. My next big test came against Argentinian opponent, Feliciano Dario Azuaga Ledezma, a veteran who had a record consisting of sixty-seven victories, only eight defeats and two draws. He was no match for my youthful exuberance and speed, crumbling in the fifth round following some damaging combinations. I truly felt invincible that night, knowing championship glory was right around the corner.

A TRUE HEART

Days after the bout, I experienced my first heartbreak. My fiancée, who I had been with for four years at the time, decided to call it quits on our relationship, a few days before my twenty-first birthday. My brother and manager, Emaid, tried to cheer me up throwing a surprise birthday dinner for me. My family, friends, trainer Harry, and boxing great Jeff Fenech, were among the guests on that special night. Jeff announced he would be taking me on a trip with him to Las Vegas to meet and train with Mike Tyson for six weeks.

This was a significant trip in terms of what it did for my boxing career. Not only did I have the chance to train alongside one of the sport's biggest stars of the previous two decades, but it also saw me sign with one of the biggest promotional companies in the world. During my time in Las Vegas, I met Joe Mir, the manager of Footlocker in Fashion Show Mall. I noticed Joe had a picture on the wall of himself with Prince Naseem Hamed, so naturally I asked how he knew Naz. He explained he was great friends with Naz and didn't believe me when I said I had lived and trained with him a number of times in the past couple of years. Joe called Naz right there, in the Footlocker, to confirm if what I had told him was true. Naz immediately told Joe Mir, 'Bilal is my little brother and he's going to become world champion very soon.'

After getting off the phone with Naz, Joe went on to tell me how he was also very close to legendary boxers, Sugar Shane Mosley and Bernard Hopkins, both of whom were stakeholders in Oscar De La Hoya's promotional company, Golden Boy Promotions. I told Mir how I had given Eric Gomez, a major player in the company, a disc with highlights from my fights. Joe offered to speak to Mosley and see if he could help me get signed to Golden Boy. All of this cultivated in a trip to Pomona, California, where I would meet Shane Mosley and ultimately be the first Australian boxer to sign with Golden Boy Promotions.

A few days before heading to Pomona, I contacted my trainer Harry to explain the turn of events. He decided he would meet me in Las Vegas and we could head to Pomona together. After a short journey, Joe Mir, Harry and I arrived and met with Mosley and his family. It was a surreal experience, and things became a whole lot more exciting when Shane asked if I was keen to go to his gym and train with him. When we arrived at the gym, Shane began to wrap his hands. 'Shane, why are you wrapping your hands?' I asked.

'So, we can spar, Billy!' he responded. I was shocked. Twenty-one years old, and here I was, standing in the opposite corner of an all-time great. To say I was nervous would be the ultimate understatement. Shane and I shared the ring for what seemed the longest four rounds of my life. I put my nervousness aside, knowing this was my one chance to impress him. What happened next changed the course of my boxing career. After getting out of the ring, Shane looked at me and said, 'How would you like to be signed to Golden Boy Promotions?' I was astounded, telling him it would be a dream come true! Shane immediately rang Oscar De La Hoya to inform him he'd be signing me, and to my surprise, Oscar already knew of me, having seen the highlights disc I'd earlier given to Eric Gomez. It was so hard to contain my excitement. I was just a kid who grew up in Engadine, a quiet suburb of Sydney, and now I was set to make my mark in the world of boxing by being signed to one of the biggest promotional companies in the sport. I was about to go from fighting in obscure venues in Australia to some of the most iconic venues boxing has ever been staged. It was a journey I will most definitely never forget.

CHAPTER FOUR
GOLDEN BOY

I made my promotional debut at the St. Pete Times Forum in Tampa, Florida, beating well-travelled journeyman, Phillip Payne, on the undercard of Ronald 'Winky' Wright vs. Ike Quartey. Two months later I was back in the squared circle at Mandalay Bay Resort and Casino in Las Vegas, this time against former world title challenger, Carlos Contreras. The bout took place on the undercard of Shane Mosley's fight against Luis Collazo. It was after this victory that Oscar De La Hoya announced his upcoming mega-bout against Floyd Mayweather Jr for the WBC Junior Middleweight Championship, in what would become one of the most anticipated events boxing had seen for decades.

At this point in my career, I was being managed by my brother, Emaid and Joey Melhem, a successful Sydney businessman. They both worked tirelessly to get me a spot on this amazing card. One day during training, I received a call with some mind-blowing news; not only had I secured a spot on the card, but I'd been invited to join Shane Mosley in Oscar's training camp in Puerto Rico. During this time, I was blessed to spar with some amazing talent. The likes of Mosley, Francisco Bojado, Rey Bautista and AJ Banal were just a few of the fighters I was able to share the ring with during the camp.

The buzz around the whole event was massive. Two of the sport's biggest stars, De La Hoya and Mayweather, were headlining an event which was set to become the highest grossing fight of all time and I was blessed to be a part of it. After a long and enjoyable camp in Puerto Rico, Shane and I headed back to Las Vegas with Oscar and his team to complete the last week of training camp. Harry, my father, Joey Melhem and a few of my siblings were there to meet us in Las Vegas. It seemed the whole city was buzzing in the days leading up to fight night. It was easily the most exciting card I had ever been a part of. I made sure I took it all in my stride, but also completely zoned in and focused on my opponent. I would be squaring up against a former IBA World Champion in Jose Alberto Gonzalez over eight rounds – a tough test at that stage of my career.

The atmosphere of the weigh-in was truly electrifying. There was a larger attendance for the weigh-in than I was used to seeing at fight nights back in Australia. Both Gonzalez and I came in under the contracted Super Featherweight limit and it was time to refuel. I couldn't wait to have the chance to impress on such a high-profile card. I was keen to showcase my skills and abilities to what promised to be a large crowd, filled with the who's who of the boxing game, as well as the Hollywood elite. Although it was hard to contain my excitement, I made sure I went to my room early that night to get a good rest.

The next night was truly special on many fronts. I boxed smartly and out-hustled my Mexican counterpart, and despite hurting my right hand in the early rounds, I earned a unanimous decision victory and impressed in what was my toughest test so far. After the fight, I iced my hand while waiting for the highly anticipated main event. The fight lived up to the hype as Mayweather and De La Hoya went back and forth for twelve rounds. Their bout went to a nail-biting split decision verdict which Mayweather claimed – only just. Whilst I was disappointed for Oscar because of my ties with his promotional company, I was still on a massive high having been part of such a special night.

At the conclusion of the post-fight talks, I made my way to Oscar's change room, and it was there I met Floyd for the first time. As he was being followed by a camera crew and a few members of his entourage, he stopped to speak to me, and his next few words astonished me. He told me I was the future of boxing, explaining he'd watched my fight in his change room and complimented me on my defence and hand speed. I was honoured to hear that from the 'pound-for-pound' best fighter in the world at the time. Floyd did all this in front of the camera crew and rap star, 50 Cent, who took some time to take some pictures with my father and me. At the end of our chat, Floyd told me to let him know when I became a free agent.

I was 16-0 and well on my way in my journey toward becoming a world champion. It felt like everything was on track and nothing could derail me from fulfilling my destiny. I headed back home with my team and soon began preparation for my next bout, scheduled against another tough Mexican warrior in Eduardo Escobedo on a Juan Manuel Marquez undercard. With another camp completed, my trainer Harry, co-manager Joey and a sponsor of mine headed to LA. During our time there, we learnt Marquez had suffered a hand injury and the whole show was being cancelled.

It was at this point my life changed forever.

Harry, who had been my trainer since my childhood, became ill and was no longer able to work my corner. He was a father-figure and mentor and had guided me throughout my whole boxing career to that point, but he was no longer there. It was a massive psychological blow for me at the time, but I had to accept he had his own personal issues to deal with and move on.

After talking with my brother, Emaid, and a few other members of my team, we decided I would join Shane Mosley and train alongside him as he prepared for his bout against Peurto Rican star, Miguel Cotto, a card which I would also fight on. For this camp, I trained under the guidance of Shane's father and trainer, Jack Mosley, as we prepared for the battle-hardened Rogers Mtagwa. It was a foreign feeling being in a new camp under a different trainer. We didn't have much time to gel and I had to deal with different ideas on how I should be trained, as well as how I should approach my upcoming bout.

Despite the early teething problems, it turned out to be a great camp. It was such a great learning experience for me as I had the opportunity to train alongside Shane, watch what it took to be at the very top of the sport and deal with being a part of a major fight. Our camp was shifted to the high-altitude setting of Big Bear, California. After ten weeks of training, another camp was wrapping up. Although I was excited, a part of me was hurting. I was about to fight on another major card at the famed Madison Square Garden for the very first time. But this time I wouldn't be sharing the experience with my long-time trainer, Harry, and I couldn't help but be nervous about it. My concerns eased throughout fight week as a few of my brothers and long-time cutman and friend, Brian Wilmott, joined us in New York. Brian had always been a major figure in my boxing career. He'd been in my corner since day one as a professional and is regarded as one of Australia's best cutmen and cornerman. He knows me very well and often gets the best out of me with just a few words.

As the bell rang, I stood centre-ring against Mtagwa in one of the most iconic venues in boxing history, Madison Square Garden. It was the very same venue my childhood hero, Prince Naseem Hamed, had knocked out Kevin Kelley in what will long be considered as one of the best featherweight championship fights – ever. Now it was my turn to make a statement against a very credible opponent. As the early rounds passed by, it was clear Mtagwa was no match for my speed and movement. His only chance of victory was to make it a rough-and-tumble battle. My new cornerman, Jack Mosley, wanted me to stay on my toes and frustrate my slower opponent and that's exactly what I did, cruising to a near shut-out victory across all the scorecards, improving my record to 17-0. Mission complete!

Once my fight was done, I made my way to my seat to watch Shane go up against Miguel Cotto. They went back and forth in a classic battle, each asserting their dominance at different times in the fight. It was somewhat a coming of age for Cotto who claimed a razor-thin unanimous decision and the biggest victory of his career thus far. The fight could have gone either way and many ringside believed Shane had done enough to win. Shane was extremely disappointed he wasn't awarded the victory but was very humble in defeat.

In the coming days, I travelled home to spend some time with my family and serve as best man at my brother Mouhammad's wedding. Only a few weeks later, I found myself in a bit of a sticky situation. I learned Jin Mosley, Shane's wife and manager at the time, felt I was a distraction to Shane and his own training. All of this meant I was once again without a trainer, and I found myself scrambling to find someone who could help me on my journey. Around this time, I was doing some conditioning work with my cutman Brian, and one day during a running session, Brian suggested that with his experience in the boxing game and our positive relationship, he could seamlessly take over my head-coaching role. I liked the idea, taking into account how comfortable I already was with Brian and the time it would take to gel with a new trainer from outside of my camp.

It was announced soon after that my next fight would take place on the undercard of fellow Australian Michael Katsidis' world title clash against Joel Casamayor in Cabazon, California. It was time to get to work. I was now training under my third different trainer in less than six months. It was far from ideal, but I knew I couldn't let anything get in the way of me reaching my dream. My opponent would come in the form of Edgar Fabian Vargas, who sported a respectable 11-3 record. In what I still consider to be one of the finer performances of my career, I battered and bruised Vargas through ten rounds in front of his home crowd. I was, and still am, bewildered as to why I was only awarded a split decision victory despite dominating my opponent. Nevertheless, my record had improved to 18-0.

CHAPTER FIVE
COMING HOME

Upon arriving back to Australia, I started looking for somewhere I could open my own personal gym, somewhere I could train whilst living in Australia in-between fights. It wasn't long before I had found the perfect location, and with the help of my brothers Emaid and Mouhammad, and best friend Morad, who we fondly nicknamed 'Panda', I was able to open and furnish the gym in very little time.

My team and I decided I should hire Australia's best-performed trainer, the legendary Johnny Lewis, as my head coach and take a few fights in Australia so we could gel in our fighter-trainer partnership. A little less than two months had passed since my last fight in America and after a short camp under the guidance of Johnny Lewis, I found myself in the ring on Australian soil for the first time in almost two years. I disposed of my opponent, Leon Maratas, with relative ease, scoring a fifth round TKO victory. My first fight under Johnny was a success and it wasn't long until I was back in the ring, this time scoring a third round TKO win over Rey Anton Olarte.

I was now 20-0 with eleven KOs and on the verge of capturing my first world championship. Having faced two southpaws in my previous two fights, I was set to face another southpaw in Zolani Marali, a tall and rangy boxer from South Africa. We would be battling for the IBO Super Featherweight World Title in Newcastle, Australia, on an Anthony 'The Man' Mundine undercard. I was stoked to have the opportunity to challenge for my first world championship on home soil.

Years earlier, I had watched Anthony capture his first world championship against Antwun Echols. To be sharing the big stage with him and co-headlining a show together was very special and I am forever grateful to Anthony for granting me the opportunity. Making things even more exciting was having Sugar Shane Mosley travel to Australia to help me prepare for the biggest night of my boxing career to date.

I travelled to Newcastle two days ahead of the fight to finish off my preparation and cut the last bit of weight. On the day of the weigh-in, it was clear to see how drained Marali was. I thought to myself at the time there was no way he could recover in twenty-four hours until our fight would take place. The day of the fight came, and with it, a flooding of emotions.

It was in the hotel room where I would break down for the first time, to my best friend, Panda. I was finding it incredibly difficult to deal with the pressure I had put on myself to win the fight and a world title. I told Panda I needed my mother, as she was the only one who could calm my nerves and I would refuse to fight unless she was in attendance. Upon hearing I was breaking down, my mother made the two-hour journey from Sydney to Newcastle and immediately came to see me when she arrived. After a good chat with her, I felt a lot better and made my way downstairs to be with the rest of my team. When the lift opened, I was greeted by a massive cheer from a number of my family and friends who had come to Newcastle to watch me fight. They began to chant my name and at that moment I broke down into tears once again. I was terrified of failing and letting my family, friends, and most of all, Shane Mosley down.

After a few positive words from Shane, we made our way to the venue where we met with my cornermen. Only moments before entering the ring, I pulled my head trainer Johnny Lewis to the side and made him promise me we wouldn't be going home without the belt.

I was then set to go to war – and that is exactly the type of fight it turned out to be. My first thought when I saw my opponent was that he looked like a different person to the drawn-out and dehydrated man I had seen the day before at the weigh-in. It was clear he had hydrated well and filled out, looking more like a junior welterweight than a super featherweight. For the first time in my career, I visited the canvas after suffering a flash knock down in the third round. From that moment on, the fight became a war of attrition, as I went back and forth with Marali, who was proving awkward and difficult for me to find my timing against. As each round passed it became more about a battle of will rather than skill, with Johnny Lewis imploring me to dig deeper than I ever had before. I did just that, digging down to a part of myself I didn't even know existed, pressing the action and taking chances against my South African counterpart. After twelve brutal rounds, the fight went to the judges' scorecards which read as follows:

116-112, 116-114 and 114-113 all for your winner, AND THE NEW IBO SUPER FEATHERWEIGHT CHAMPION OF THE WORLD ... BILLY 'THE KID' DIB!!

What a feeling! My dream had come true and I was finally a world champion after so many years of hard work and dedication to the sport of boxing. The feeling I had that night is somewhat unexplainable; a state of ecstasy coming over me as I realised I had achieved a lifelong goal.

I was so proud to have made my family, friends and fans so happy. A young boy who was bullied at school was now on top of the world. A vivid memory was having Billy Hussein come into my change room to congratulate me. I reminded Billy of the time many years beforehand where he told me winning a world title would be a massive task. When I told Billy, he responded by telling me I'd have to win one of the major world championship belts to be right.

A week or so after my bout against Marali, the IBO contacted my team to inform us the Marali camp had lodged a protest, believing he had done enough to win the fight. Upon review, the IBO decided to order an immediate rematch between Marali and me. At that stage, we had already been in contact with my promotional company, Golden Boy Promotions, who had advised me there was a much bigger opportunity on the horizon and my team decided I should vacate the title. Of course, this was disappointing, but I had to trust in the process, knowing I was moving on to bigger and better things.

CHAPTER SIX
MY FIRST DEFEAT

Golden Boy came good on their promise, delivering me a world title shot against the reigning WBO Featherweight World Champion, Steve Luevano. This was an opportunity to win a second world title in a second division, and although it came at short notice, the appeal of having a chance to become a two-weight world champion meant it was too good to pass up on. The fight would also be televised on one of the largest television networks, HBO, taking place on the undercard of Bernard Hopkins vs. Kelly Pavlik. Whilst I knew my decision to vacate the IBO World Title would be met with some criticism, it was a pretty easy decision to make given what was at stake.

The date was set for 18 October 2008, meaning I had less than seven weeks in total to prepare for another twelve-round battle. Whilst this wasn't ideal, I felt it was enough time and was spurred on by the prospect of holding the exact same WBO World Title Prince Naseem once held.

Training camp commenced and I had a fair bit of weight to lose in order to make the contracted featherweight limit of 57.2kg. I was working hard under the watchful eye of Johnny Lewis when an outstanding opportunity presented itself. At a meeting for potential sponsorship, I was met with a surprise when I was asked if I would like to have my original trainer, Harry Hammoud, back in my camp.

Nora, the owner of Prize Fighter and a potential sponsor, was Harry's sister. At our meeting she asked what I thought of having Harry return to my camp once again. I was quick to jump at the opportunity, but telling Nora I would first need to speak with my current trainer about bringing Harry in to help. Johnny was accommodating when I did approach him and he was completely understanding, realising the relationship Harry and I had built over the past ten years or so. Just like that, Harry was back, and it felt as if he'd never left, as he and Johnny worked together to get me ready for the biggest fight of my career.

I was back in the gym with my trainers, Harry and Johnny. To help me prepare for Luevano's southpaw style, my team flew in Fred Tukes from America. Fred was a good friend of mine who I met on camp with Shane Mosley. A southpaw, Fred was a renowned sparring partner and had worked with some of the best fighters in the world. Upon his arrival to Australia, we immediately got to work, formulating a solid game plan for the fight. The game plan, however, was not my biggest battle. The real battle was making the featherweight limit, a weight class I hadn't made since 2006, two years earlier.

One week out from the fight, my team and I flew out to Atlantic City, New Jersey, where the fight would take place. It was torturous, as I spent the whole week drying out my body, struggling to get under the weight limit of 57.2kg. On the morning of the weigh-in, I woke up with 1.1kg to lose, so I had to will myself through a light jog before doing some pad work with Harry.

The toughest battle before the weigh-in is the time spent in the sauna. Already severely dehydrated, the heat of the sauna felt unbearable at times. A few hours ahead of the weigh-in, I had successfully made the featherweight limit and breathed a massive sigh of relief.

The day of the fight arrived and I was in good spirits knowing I had the chance to make history. I had the sort of confidence you would expect a young, undefeated fighter to have, especially one coming off his first-ever world championship victory.

Whilst I felt there was significant pressure to perform, I was as relaxed as I had ever been in the hours leading up to the fight. It was my time to announce myself as a legitimate world champion to the American audience and major television network, HBO.

Unfortunately, it wasn't meant to be, and I suffered my first-ever defeat as a professional. Luevano used his experience and championship pedigree, beating me to the punch on most occasions and never allowing me to gather any serious momentum. After a tactical twelve-round battle, deemed 'lacklustre' and 'boring', I eventually lost to a competitive unanimous decision via the scores of 115-113, 116-112 and 117-111.

I was devastated, realising I had missed out on my piece of history as well as an amazing opportunity to impress the boxing world. Walking back to the change rooms, heartbroken with tears flowing, I was comforted by my brother, Emaid, who told me he was proud of me and how far I'd come. It was in those moments in the change room where I realised everyone loves a winner, and only your true loved ones will be there for you when you're not in the winning column.

This was my first-ever defeat as a professional boxer. It wasn't easy to take.

Searching for answers in the change room, the team had a quick debrief and Emaid was honest without being too critical. 'You didn't have the killer instinct tonight, the "Eye of the Tiger",' he said. That was probably the hardest thing to deal with at the time, knowing I didn't leave absolutely everything I had out there for the first time in my career, on my most important night.

The flight home to Sydney was long and painful, as I pondered on what could have been. I thought about the reception I'd have gotten if I was coming home a winner rather than a loser. Instead, I arrived at Sydney Airport, welcomed home by most of my family and loved ones which was heartening. Still, the next few days I felt completely empty and spent them crying on my mother's lap. As I mentioned earlier, you learn about the ones who truly care about you after a loss, and I was blessed with a few people who would do their best to cheer me up. A phone call from Naz after the fight lit a fire in my belly, with his words, 'Get ready – because the comeback is greater than the setback,' ringing in my ears.

CHAPTER SEVEN
THE REBUILD

The most important person in your boxing career is undoubtedly your trainer. The bond between a fighter and their trainer should be strong and the chemistry must be there. I couldn't help but feel the bond I once shared with Harry was no longer there and I had some hard decisions to make. A few weeks after the loss to Luevano, we cut our ties. Although it was the second time around, it wasn't easy. Harry wasn't just my trainer, he was a father-figure to me. We cut ties respectfully and have remained friends and in contact with each other since that day. I consider him a lifelong friend and will never forget the times we had.

Rebuilding after a defeat is no easy task. The ego takes a massive dent and many nights are spent doubting yourself. I would be forced back to the drawing board, but I was still young – only twenty-three years old. I knew time was on my side, but I would have to make a lot of changes in myself to reach the heights I wanted to reach; it wasn't just my boxing style I needed to change, but myself as a person too. Coming to grips with that is difficult, but I learnt quickly how boxing can strip you down as quickly as it builds you up.

As I pondered change, I received a phone call that altered my life forever. The phone call was from the Saudi Arabian Embassy who were extending me an invitation to take part in the Islamic Pilgrimage to the holy city of Mecca, referred to as 'Hajj'. Whilst I was honoured, I was unsure if I was ready to do the Hajj and politely declined the offer. My initial reluctance was met with anger from my mother. 'You are turning down an invitation to visit the house of God in the holy city?' She explained to me it would be a great opportunity to do some soul-searching and to connect with God. She mentioned that at Mount Arafat, an integral part of Hajj, my 'Duaa' (supplication) would be accepted by God and made true. I took my mother's advice and set upon my journey to Saudi Arabia; a journey I was told to call 'the labour of love'. For me though, it was a journey where I could truly find myself, a journey that would change my life forever.

As I stood on the Mountain of Arafat, I felt guilty and ashamed; the only thing I was planning to ask Allah SWT, was to help me win a world championship. I thought I should be praying for those who were less fortunate than me. Those who went without. Those who were oppressed. Those who could only ever dream of living the life I was blessed with.

So those prayers came first and foremost. I then asked Allah to guide me to someone who could help me reach my dream of becoming a champion but only if it was of a benefit to myself and to other people.

Although I was without a trainer at the time, I made sure I was back in the gym as soon as I could. Johnny Lewis had so many responsibilities and wasn't able to train me at my gym, so I was on the look out for a new trainer.

One morning I met with Hussein Hussein, a great boxer who had represented Australia at the Olympics and challenged for a number of world titles throughout his professional career. After a solid session, Hussy and I sat to have a chat. I explained to him I had no trainer and was unsure of the direction to take in my career. He suggested I speak with his brother, Billy Hussein, a well-renowned trainer in Australian boxing circles. Billy was on quite a hot streak and was known to get the best out of the fighters he trained.

For some reason, I was reluctant and told Hussy there wasn't much of a chance of that happening. Billy and I had known each other for many years, dating back to my amateur boxing days, but I never thought he would ever be interested in training me. Hussy told me he'd speak to Billy and could persuade him to train me.

A few days later, I met with Billy Hussein for our first session. Our styles were contrasting at the start. Billy was asking me to do things I had never done in my career. 'Bend your legs. Get low. You're safest there!' These were cues I wasn't used to hearing as I was put through a gruelling session of intense bag and pad work. Billy was very much a defensive-minded coach and he told me I would have to improve defensively if I wanted to prolong my career.

After the session was complete, Billy explained he liked the prospect of training me, saying many people had written me off after my loss, but he wanted to prove they had yet to see the best of me.

But rules would need to be put in place in order for Billy to take over as my head trainer.

He explained he would need ten fights to help rebuild me into a championship-level fighter. He made it known he would not take part in any world title fights before we had seen out the ten. His rules and expectations were set out. He then asked if I had any expectations of my own. I asked Billy if we could train in my own gym, one on one, and the other thing I would ask of him was to guide me to a world championship, promising him I would do 'whatever it takes'.

Now we had both agreed, we shook hands and started our journey towards a world championship. Our first assignment together was to derail the career of undefeated rising star, the late Davey Browne Jr, who held an unblemished record of fifteen wins and one draw. He was the reigning WBC Youth Champion and IBF Pan Pacific Champion. A win over Davey could catapult my name back into the world rankings.

The ten-week long camp was one I will remember forever, as Billy Hussein transformed me into a well-rounded fighter, rather than just a pretty and slick boxer. Whilst a lot of what we worked on was foreign to me, I was beginning to reap the rewards of the work we put in and by the time fight night came around, I was ready to show the world the new version of Billy Dib was a force to be reckoned with.

On the night 11 March 2009, I proved just that, earning a great victory over Davey Browne Jr. Billy had formulated a plan to bully Davey, and I followed the plan to a tee. I out-hustled and mugged my opponent before a cut caused by an accidental head clash forced the bout to be stopped and we went to the scorecards. I truly felt I was on a different level that night, enjoying the changes that were made throughout camp, comfortably earning a technical decision victory once the scorecards were read. I was elated to be back in the winners' circle once again. Topping off a great night was the fact I felt Billy and I had clicked on fight night. It was my first fight under Billy's guidance and I was impressed by his calm nature in the corner which allowed him to deliver concise instructions. Our plan to get to another world championship bout was on track.

CHAPTER EIGHT
CHARGE TO THE WORLD TITLE

In the lead-up to world championship glory, I scored nine victories in ten fights, with eight of those victories coming inside the distance. This wasn't before a minor speed bump, however. My very next bout, after scoring a solid victory over Davey Browne, was deemed a no contest. I was headlining a show held in one of Sydney's most iconic amusement parks against Japan's Kenichi Yamaguchi – an unforgettable night for both me and Australian boxing as a whole!

The fight started at a wild pace, as the awkward Yamaguchi chased me around the ring. Before a minute had even elapsed, I was pushed to the canvas and collected in the face by my opponent's knee. What happened after was a complete blur to me, only realising what happened after reviewing the footage from the fight. Still shaken from the knee in the face, I was knocked down once again and sought to get through the round. Before the end of the round, I knocked Yamaguchi to the canvas too but regretfully punched him while he was down. Unfortunately, the referee, Les Fear, did not see the illegal blow and began his count on Yamaguchi after ushering me to the neutral corner. Although Yamaguchi beat the count, he appeared unsteady, leading the referee to call a halt to the bout. I truly wish I could have the next few moments back. Whilst Yamaguchi was fuming at the referee's decision, I was celebrating with my corner. I turned around and saw Yamaguchi coming toward me and instinctively pushed him away and then pushed his trainer away who had come to get in the middle of us. This unfortunately sparked a small commotion in the ring between our two teams. When things calmed down, I was eventually announced as the winner via first-round TKO. The decision was changed to a no contest by the NSW Boxing Authority less than a month later, after they deemed that Yamaguchi was struck by an accidental but illegal punch whilst on the canvas. I accepted the decision made and moved on as quickly as possible.

I was back into the gym right away, eager to erase the memory of the Yamaguchi fight. I had to put the unfortunate episode behind me and the only way to do so was to move forward. In the ensuing twelve months, I fought as regularly as possible whilst working my way up the world rankings. During this stretch of fights, I scored seven victories, winning six of them by KO, highlighted by a few key victories against some well-credentialed fighters, such as Reynaldo Belandres, Wacharakrit Senahan and Ceferino Dario Labarda. Labarda was an Argentinian Olympian whose only previous defeat had come against Steve Molitor, the IBF Super Bantamweight Champion. I disposed of Labarda quite handily, forcing him to retire on his stool after what was described as a 'bashing' by the Fox Sports commentary team. That night had me feeling somewhat invincible. The work Billy Hussein and

I had been putting in at the gym was paying dividends on fight night and for the first time in a long time I felt I was a complete fighter, ready to be back on the world stage. Billy reminded me to stay on course, telling me that whilst it was an impressive performance against a credible opponent, we had to stay on par with our plan of having ten fights before we moved on to a world title fight.

I tore through another two opponents in quick succession after the Labarda fight, stopping future IBO Super Featherweight World Champion, Jack Asis, in the fourth round and dominating Australian veteran Mick 'Pony' Shaw on route to an eighth-round TKO victory.

I was now 9-0 with one no contest under the guidance of Billy Hussein and had climbed up to number five in the IBF Featherweight World Rankings. Things were aligning nicely as I pushed ahead towards world championship glory, however, I had one final hurdle to overcome against hardened Filipino, Ricky Sismundo. Sismundo had an impressive record of twenty wins from twenty-five fights and had previously pushed some very good boxers to their limits. We would square off at the WA Italian Club in Perth, Western Australia, on a CDL Boxing Promotions card. I was followed to Perth by a number of family, friends and members of my team and was excited to put on a great performance, sensing a world title bout would be next, just as Billy and I had planned. Sismundo proved a worthy opponent, coming all night long as I teed off on him. Whilst I was comfortably ahead on the cards, I was still fighting with a sense of urgency, knowing I was on a streak of six straight KO victories. Ahead of the eighth and final round, Billy asked me to be cautious and not do anything which could jeopardise my impending shot at a world title. I reminded him of my KO streak and told him I couldn't do that, choosing instead to push the pace, earning a stoppage victory to keep my KO streak alive and cap off a memorable trip.

I had well and truly put the demons of my lone loss to Steve Luevano behind me and could feel something special was about to happen to my career. Days after my victory over Sismundo, Yuriorkis Gamboa, the IBF Featherweight World Champion, was stripped of his title after failing to comply with the mandatory re-weigh on fight day. Whilst he secured a stoppage victory over his opponent, the IBF Featherweight title was now vacant. When the IBF Featherweight World Rankings for March 2011 were released, I was rated at number four and a world title bout against Mexican/American superstar Mikey Garcia, rated number two at the time, seemed likely, as we were the two highest-rated contenders.

Before Billy Hussein agreed to take on the challenge of rebuilding my career, he'd had a few requests. His number one was he would need ten fights to rebuild me before we would take on the challenge of trying to capture another world championship.

Billy had done an excellent job guiding me to ten wins recording eight stoppages along the way; my career was moving in the right direction.

In 2008, I had stood on the mountain of Arafat in Makkah asking the Almighty to lead me to a team who could guide me to another world championship. My prayers were answered. In the weeks that followed my victory over Sismundo, a man who had been instrumental in my rebuild, Mike Altamura, called me with the great news that a world championship was knocking on my door.

Things began to get interesting; my chance to win a championship had arrived. My opponent was to be Mikey Garcia. With Mike Altamura deep in negotiations with Mikey Garcia's management, a deal looked likely to happen on our terms. I had a strong team on the negotiating table, including my brother, Emaid, and successful businessman

Mike K. Mike, a wealthy man determined to make this fight happen for me on home soil.

After weeks of back and forth, negotiations broke down with promotor Top Rank deciding to take Mikey in another direction. Top Rank decided to use my lacklustre showing against Luevano against me, labelling me unsellable. The truth was, they would have never won the purse bid and couldn't afford to send a star like Mikey to Australia. I aimed to bring the fight to Australia to give myself the best opportunity to win it. I knew facing Mikey in America would be an uphill battle as he was being established as a future star.

Next in line was the highest contender, Jorge Lacierva. Negotiations were smooth, and a date with destiny was set for Friday 29 July 2011.

Jorge was a solid competitor who had appeared in two championship bouts losing to both Mark 'Too Sharp' Johnson and Celestino Caballero who had made an impressive eleven title defences of his WBA World Championship.

Jorge had an impressive thirty-nine victories with twenty-six KOs alongside seven losses and six draws. He was on a seven-fight win streak heading into our bout. With camp officially set, a team was assembled, with significant momentum coming into camp as I had lived in the gym since 2008.

The camp was broken into three blocks consisting of four weeks per block; part of the camp was spent in the Gold Coast where we lived and trained at the home of Mike K. I had world-class sparring on hand, which helped in perfecting the game plan to a tee. Eight weeks out from fight date, Billy Hussein sent me a text message which took my intensity to another level. The exact statement read as:

B everything so far has been great. I now ask you to give these eight weeks your full attention and dedication. With Allah's permission and help

I'm going to make you the IBF World Champ Inn Sha Allah. I have so much faith in you, bro. You're now the complete package it's getting harder as of Monday be ready. PROUD OF YOU BROTHER

After receiving this message, nothing but God's decree would stop me from winning this championship. I was prepared in a way of knowing all I had to do was turn up and I would be victorious.

Training camp was smooth sailing – from media training sessions to short documentaries being filmed following the incredible journey.

We couldn't cut a deal with Fox Sports to air my fight, so we struck a deal with MAINEVENT TV to air it on delayed telecast. I did not allow this to worry me as I was focused on the task at hand. The show was being promoted by BILLY THE KID entertainment in association with Michael K.

Our fabulous sponsors and James Packer's generosity ensured my dream of becoming a world champion would soon become a reality.

On 27 July 2011, I would come face to face with the man who stood in my way of winning my second championship. At the press conference, I spoke of the opportunity of winning the IBF crown on home soil.

Billy Hussein mentioned to the media that he felt he had the right kid (BTK) to beat any of the current champions at this point. Lacierva was asked how he felt, and his response was, 'One thing I can guarantee is you're going to see a great fight. I came here to give everything as every Mexican does. We have big pride, and I hope not to disappoint.'

When asked about our predictions, my response was, 'I'm not going to disrespect my opponent and say I'm going to knock him out. I will say I'm going to put on a great performance, and at the end of the bout, my hand will be raised in victory. I'll save Jorge the extra luggage and keep the world title belt here in Australia.'

28 July was weigh-in day. Emotions were flying high as fight night

was only one sleep away. Making the featherweight limit of 57.1kg was a breeze. I was ripped and ready, as was Jorge. The face-off was a little heated as Jorge got up in my space and placed his hand on my face, pushing it to intimidate me. But I could see the fear in his eyes. As the weigh-in took place in the Top Ryde Shopping Centre, the excitement was present with many onlookers.

CHAPTER NINE
A LIFE-CHANGING MOMENT

The moment had arrived. I was completely relaxed and focused on the task at hand. All the years of hard work were about to pay dividends. During the day, I visited Lakemba Mosque, where the Mufti introduced me and asked all those present to join in a prayer that I would be victorious. I was calm and relaxed as I assured my brother, Emaid, I had no doubt I would be victorious on the night. Before heading to the venue, I stopped by to see my mother who told me a story that would make the hair on my neck and arms stand up. She spoke of when she was leaving the hospital after having given birth to me, and walking past a pious, older man, he stopped my parents and asked if it was a boy who was in the pram. He asked my mother and father if he could see me, and of course they responded. After looking at me, this wise-looking man told my mother and father, 'Someday your son will be someone who inspires others, someone who is famous.' My mother had asked if I might be a premier someday, and the man had laughed, saying, 'I'm not sure, but he will be famous.'

I shed tears of joy knowing I would come good on his promise and I would be known as one of the best featherweights in the world.

We headed to the venue. I was cool, calm and collected as I walked into the change room. I remember it clearly. The room was filled with all those I loved and who had played a part in my journey towards this great opportunity; my father, brothers, my cousins, my dearest friend Adam Houda, and the man who had helped guide me to the championship, Billy Hussein.

The atmosphere was electric, but the calmness was present, as I rehearsed over and over again what we had worked on in the long weeks of camp leading into this life-changing moment. As a team, we always got together moments before I was called out to the squared circle; this time my father gave a very powerful prayer.

Billy Hussein added, 'Do not be distracted. Keep your eyes on your opponent only. No-one else exists. It's just you and Lacierva. He's coming to your home to take your title.'

'No way,' I responded.

'It's a big insult. The time for talk is over. I don't need to motivate you. I've heard about what you're going to do for the last fourteen weeks. DO IT.'

As I walked to the ring, Perry Cale announced, 'And now ... ladies and gentlemen, please welcome the Lebanese Lethario, the Master of Disaster, the Prince of Persia, the Charismatic Enigma, the Count of Monte Fisto, the Lightning of Liverpool, the Guru of Greenacre, the Duke of Demolition, the Earl of Enforcement, the Chosen One, the King of Kings, the Terminator of Tripoli ... every day he's shuffling. Ladies and gentlemen, representing Australia, the one, the only … Billy "The Kid" Dib!!!!'

We meet in centre ring and touch gloves as the referee gives his final instructions. Back to the corner for a final hug from Billy H, he instructs me to keep my right hand up. The bell rings and the fight is underway.

I open the bought confidently behind a fast jab as Jorge rushes his way in, trying to bully me. Everything we've discussed and worked on during training is falling into place. Jorge is growing more and more frustrated as none of his punches land with any significance.

Only two or three rounds into the bout and dirty tactics are coming into play. Lacierva is trying everything to upset me but all I can hear is Billy Hussein's words. 'Be calm … He's only getting dirty because he can't hit you.'

As the bout progresses, I continue to score with flurries of punches, banking round after round on the judges' scorecards. Billy is extremely happy and asks me to stay on course, to stay focused and ensure my hand will be raised in victory and I will be crowned champion.

Going into the last two rounds, instead of cruising to victory, I look to press the action and score a stoppage victory. And although I comfortably win the last two rounds, the knockout does not come. We are forced to go to the scorecards.

'Ladies and gentlemen … after twelve rounds of action, we go to the judges' score cards. It is a unanimous decision.'

Charlie Lucas – 119/109. Alejandro Lopez – 118/109. Somsak Sirianant – 115/112

'The winner, from Australia, and the new IBF champion of the world – Billy "The Kid" Dib.'

Hearing those words, I can't tell you how relieved I am. All my hard work has paid off. Once again, I am champion of the world.

Winning the IBO World Title was great but winning the IBF

World Title placed me in the history books as a legitimate world champion. Writing these words had me in tears. Thinking about that life-changing moment took me back to the overwhelming feelings of pride and achievement.

Saturday 30 July 2011, I woke up as the featherweight champion of the world. The feeling was unexplainable. With the month of Ramadan a few days away, my father organised a family barbecue and invited each and every person who had been involved in making my dream a reality. Media attention was becoming something of the norm. Day in, day out I was receiving great coverage. As the saying goes 'everybody loves a winner'.

During the month of Ramadan, I received many invites to break my fast with honourable members of the Arab community who were ever so proud of me.

I was so humbled to be their champion. It felt good to feel the love from all those who were super proud of me. I was determined to keep my championship crown and defend it many times.

During the lead-up to my world championship bout with Jorge Lacierva, my cousin Ahmed, 'baby face', worked tirelessly by helping the promotional team sell tickets and attending all my training sessions to make sure I was looked after.

I had made a promise to my cousin, if I was successful in capturing the championship, I would take him on a trip to Las Vegas. I stayed true to my word, and after the month of Ramadan, we booked our flights – 'Vegas bound, baby.'

I had been working so hard since 2008, perfecting my style and staying consistent by being a gym rat, as my only focus was to capture world championship glory. Now, I felt the trip to Vegas was much deserved. This was to be only the second time my cousin had ever left Australia, making it a truly memorable trip alongside our friends Harry and Peter.

During our time in Las Vegas, we decided to attend the Floyd Mayweather vs. Victor Ortiz grand arrivals at the MGM Grand. When Floyd entered the MGM Grand lobby everyone cheered. It was mayhem. As Floyd circled the floor, he walked past my good friend Peter Mitrevski, who managed to get his attention letting him know I was now world champion. Floyd stopped to take a picture with me and said his team would be in touch. Nevertheless, my cousin and I, alongside Pete and Harry were happy to get a picture with Floyd and continue on with our holiday.

Something deep down told me Floyd would stay true to his word. After a memorable holiday we arrived back into Sydney, as plans got underway for my first world title defence. This bout would be a voluntary defence, so I was free to pick somebody from the top ten IBF rankings.

This job would be left to Billy Hussein, Emaid and my advisor, Mike Altamura. The date had been locked in. My world title defence was to be 18 November 2011.

CHAPTER TEN
FIRST WORLD TITLE DEFENCE

After more than eight weeks out of the gym, I had ballooned up to a whopping 67kg, placing me exactly 10kg over the featherweight limit. This was the first time in my career I had ever been this heavy. With a ten-week prep in my sights, I believed getting the weight off would be easy. Boy, was I wrong. My opponent was set: current European EBU champion, Alberto Servidei. He boasted an undefeated record consisting of thirty-one wins, seven KOs and two draws.

I felt the bout would be a good test as Alberto was the EBU champ, and to top it off, he was a southpaw. With all the logistics in place, we got to work on trying to secure a TV date for my first world title defence.

During this time, boxing shows would be tendered out, so we forwarded our show to Fox Sports, only to hear they had decided to go with another promotion. I was shocked, hurt and angry. I felt so disrespected. Here I was, one of only two world champions in Australia and I couldn't get my fight aired on free-to-air TV.

It was time to call upon Australian media heavy-hitter, Alan Jones. After calling Alan and explaining the situation, he stressed he wouldn't let this happen as he felt it was a travesty and an insult to me *and* Australian boxing. His exact words were … 'Don't you do or say anything silly, it will all be sorted within twenty-four hours.'

And just like that, with the help of Alan Jones, it was resolved. He secured a special edition of boxing to be televised on Saturday 19 November.

The journey was now set, dropping those 10kg I had put on during the month of Ramadan and my trip to the US. Camp was underway and everything was running smoothly. I had fantastic sparring with my southpaw teammate and 2008 Olympian, Paul Fleming.

The biggest challenge during this camp was dropping the excessive weight I had piled on since winning my championship. With only one week left in camp I still had to lose 5kg.

On the morning of the weigh-in, I woke with 1.5kg still to lose. The problem was, I was already 100% dry. I tried to rest throughout the day and with only hours left to the weigh-in and 1kg to lose, I was in trouble. We hit panic buttons. My nutritionist was shocked but had one more idea up his sleeve. He suggested I run a super-hot bath. He told me it would be hard to cope with, but if I could handle it for ten minutes, the weight would come off.

I was determined to keep my title by any means necessary. With my cousin Ahmed by my side, I got into the hot bath. It was burning. After eight long minutes I could no longer handle the heat. With the help of Ahmed, I tried to stand, only to collapse onto the floor. I began to dry-retch, feeling as though death was on my doorstep. Weak and completely depleted, I found a way to get myself together and check my weight. I stepped on the scales, and by the grace of God, they read 57kg.

I was so relieved yet very tired and fragile. I tried my best to freshen up. Adam Houda picked me up and drove me to the weigh-in which was taking place in the Italian Forum at Leichardt.

We thought that doing the weigh-in at the Italian Forum would work well for ticket sales as my opponent was Italian himself. With Alberto first to the scales making weight, my turn had now come.

With barely any energy, I slowly stepped onto the scales. Seeing the numbers 57kg bought me so much relief. Alberto and I then stood face-to-face in the final stare-down.

Now, it was time to refuel. My nutritionist had my food prepared but I was in no condition to eat; I was feeling so sick.

It wasn't until 9pm that evening that I began to feel better. One of the perks of fighting at home is having the luxury of heading to the venue and scoping it out before the fight. I got in the ring and danced around it a little, shaking off all the nerves I had been feeling.

On fight day, I was feeling 100% again. Deep down, I knew if this fight was to go the distance, cutting so much weight might come back to bite me later in the fight.

The morning of the fight, Alberto and I once again met for the mandatory IBF second weigh-in. It's mandatory we weigh no more than 10% of the 57kg weight limit. After making weight for the second time, I felt it best I spent the day with my nutritionist to ensure I stayed replenished.

At 5pm that evening, we headed to the venue where I had previously won the IBF crown. This time I was heading back for my first world title defence. My friends, family and the team who had helped me get to this point surrounded me. Before stepping out to the arena, traditionally my father would say a prayer and set me on my way. As I was about to step out of the change room, Billy Hussein pulled me back and gave me one final instruction, 'I want you to knock Alberto out in one round.'

I made my way to the stage where I would be introduced into the ring accompanied by RnB artist Stan Walker. Before stepping in the ring I stopped as Adam gave me a hug and sent me on my way. The ring announcer read out both our résumés – and the fight was on.

The first bell rang and I opened the bout confidently, landing many flush blows. Midway into the first round I landed a blow that sent Alberto to the canvas. Oddly enough, the referee declared it a slip and no knock-down was registered. I smelt the blood and saw the fear in Alberto's eyes. He was ready to go. Billy Hussein called for me to press him. With no time left in the first round, I knocked Alberto Servidei down with a vicious left rip which sat him down for the ten count.

My first world title defence was a major success. KO in round one over an unbeaten European champion. There was no better feeling than being called the champ – again!

In the post-fight interview, I looked directly into the camera lens and challenged long-time reigning WBA Featherweight World Champion, Chris John, to a unification bout, but nothing would eventuate from it.

I headed back to the change room where the celebrations got underway. My victory bought my family and friends so much joy.

CHAPTER ELEVEN
NEXT STEPS

It would be four months before I stepped back into the ring. This time it was against a man the IBF had mandated as my next opponent. The bout would take place in the state of Tasmania. It would be the first time in Australian boxing history that two Aussies would defend their IBF crowns on the same bill.

Both Daniel Geale and I had been developed through the amateur system and were no strangers to each other. We had lived at the Australian Institute of Sport and represented Australia at many tournaments around the world.

My opponent was a man I was very familiar with, as I was supposed to have fought him back in 2007 on a Golden Boy promotion to be headlined by the great Juan Manuel Marquez vs. Joel Casamayor. The show hadn't materialised and the bout was cancelled after Marquez suffered a bad hand injury. My opponent was to be Eduardo Escobedo, a hardened Mexican with an outstanding thirty-two victories alongside twenty-three KOs and three defeats. His last loss was five years back in 2007 against WBO World Champion Daniel Ponce De Leon.

This was not going to be an easy match-up, as Escobedo was on an eleven-fight winning streak, knocking seven of the eleven opponents out on his way back to the mandatory position. To top it off, he was trained by hall of fame trainer Nacho Beristain, a man who had guided many champions including the great Juan Manuel Marquez, who had been in many memorable fights with the legendary Manny Pacquiao.

Billy Hussein had another great preparation scheduled. We travelled to the United States for some world-class sparring, as we wanted to be sure to leave no stone unturned in this career-defining fight. We worked with some world-class fighters such as Sharif Bogere, Diego Magdeleno and his brother Jessie Magdeleno who would go on to become a world champion himself. But the most competitive sparring would be against two-weight world champion, Celestino Caballero, who towered over me at 180cm tall. The sparring sessions were brutal, to say the least. Celestino was a very experienced competitor who managed to bring the best out in me. Our spars generated great excitement in the gym. During our time in Vegas, we also had the opportunity to visit the team at top rank about the possibility of signing a lucrative deal, and although this never eventuated, it was a great feeling to be recognised by a powerhouse promotional company like Top Rank.

After a great few weeks in Las Vegas, we arrived back in Australia with six weeks left in camp until the showdown with Escobedo. I was in great condition and continued to show good consistency in the gym, remaining 100% focused. Three days prior to the bout, a press conference took place. Escobedo didn't speak much English so a translator was on hand to relay his message to me. He said I was a fighter, 'Who boxed like a girl.' He labelled me a runner. 'I will hunt you down and knock you out.'

I smiled and replied, 'We will see.' After our face-off, I made my way to the elevator, and by chance, Escobedo would enter the elevator just as it was going back to ground level. He had no idea what he was walking into. I was in the elevator with Adam Houda, who jokingly offered Eduardo some cake, as he looked like he was struggling with the weight cut. Adam would further taunt Eduardo by telling him this fight could be fought in a telephone booth, and not to run, as I was coming directly at him as soon as the first bell was rung. I laughed as Adam had given up my game plan. Good thing Escobedo didn't understand what Adam was saying!

On the morning of the fight, Escobedo and I crossed paths once again, this time at the twelve-hour mandatory weigh-in. Shortly after, I headed to the breakfast room and I couldn't believe what I was seeing. Escobedo was eating as though he had never seen food in his life. The only thought that crossed my mind was, *I am going to destroy this man's body tonight.* He would not be able to stand up to the onslaught, especially with all that food in his stomach.

It was fight time and as I made my way to the squared-circle, I stopped to hug my father and Adam Houda, as I had previously done in all my fights. It was somewhat of a pre-fight ritual for me, I got into the ring as the announcer read our résumés. We touched gloves and the fight was on. At the opening bell, I aggressively attacked Escobedo's body, staying true to Adam's words that this bout would be fought at phone booth range. Many of the early exchanges were wild; some of the punches would go astray, as Escobedo kept bending awkwardly low.

I wanted to show that even though Escobedo was the number-one contender, I was on a different level to him. Escobedo would land his first significant punch in round four when he caught me with a beautifully timed left hook. I was stunned but managed to stay on my feet and continued to apply constant pressure. During the break after round five, Billy Hussein ordered me to continue to put constant pressure on, promising me Escobedo was nearly done. 'Look at him,' Billy screamed. The bell rang and I pressed the action. Body blow followed body blow and I could hear Escobedo wincing. He was tough, but not even he could withstand the onslaught. The bell rang again and we headed back to our corners. *What do I have to do to stop this guy?* I thought to myself. His corner then signalled to the referee they were done. I had forced a tough Mexican, who was the number-one contender, to quit. 'NO MAS.'

After being announced the winner, Escobedo told me, through his translator, that my body attack was vicious. I explained that after seeing him at breakfast, I knew his body would not hold up to my body shots with what he had fed himself.

At the post-fight press conference, Gary Shaw, the co-promoter of the event, even said, 'This was a great performance, Billy. You should be considered a real threat as Mexicans are warriors who don't usually quit.'

I had truly arrived on the world stage. There was no doubt about it. I was on a mission to be remembered as one of the best fighters ever developed in Australia.

In the history books of boxing, there were not many Arab Muslim world champions. I was truly proud to be recognised alongside the great Prince Hamed as one of them.

My reign as featherweight champion, from 2011-2013, was some of the best years of my life. So many exciting things took place during that time, so much love and recognition from the boxing world and my community. I truly felt so special.

My goal as champion was to remain as active as I could and to have nothing less than three fights a year. So after the win against Eduardo, I was back in the gym working on my craft, while my team looked to secure my next world title defence.

CHAPTER TWELVE
COLLISION COURSE

The date was set for 13 July 2012, in a show to be co-headlined by both Joel Brunker and myself, in a bid for an all-Australian showdown between two former competitors. We were both set to face Mexican warriors, in separate bouts, with a vision we would both be victorious, leading us to an eventual showdown.

I had history with Joel. We had met many years ago in an amateur bout which I comprehensively won back in 2003. During my preparation against Lacierva, Joel had helped me with many rounds of sparring.

But before a showdown with Joel could be organised, I needed to secure a victory against a flashy Mexican southpaw by the name of Juan Antonio Rodriguez, who boasted an outstanding twenty-one wins with nineteen KOs and only three defeats.

This bout was scheduled to take place in the super featherweight limit and would be fought over ten rounds. Even though it was a non-title bout, a loss to Rodriguez could result in me being stripped of the featherweight crown I had worked so hard to defend. To ensure victory, I prepared with the mindset this was to be a world title defence.

In the lead-up to the bout with Juan, discussions surfaced about a possible future showdown with fast-rising slick American southpaw, Gary Russell Jr. The bout with Juan would serve as a great test, with a big cherry to come if I could secure a victory.

The bout with Juan would take place at a catchweight of 59kg. This would mean I could concentrate more on the prep, rather than drying myself to make the featherweight limit I was accustomed to.

After every bout I always tried to reward myself with some sort of holiday. This time I had organised a trip to Dubai, to spend time with my childhood hero, featherweight legend Prince Naseem Hamed.

On 12 July 2012, it was weigh-in day and I was exactly on the catchweight limit of 59kg. Seeing Juan was interesting. It was hard to keep a game face, as he was such a cool guy. He was extremely funny, cracking jokes at the weigh-in, but in a way I felt he may be trying to play mind games to soften me up, so I tried to keep it as professional as possible.

The bout was to be staged at the Campsie Orion Centre. It was a smaller venue than I'd been accustomed to fighting in, but I felt we would have a more intimate crowd, creating a great atmosphere. I wasn't wrong – it was electric. The show was stacked with a great undercard. On show, was the rising talent in Australian boxing, as well as my next possible opponent, Joel Brunker, who had survived a ten-round war with his Mexican rival. He got the job done, now it was my turn. After a solid warm-up, I took to the stage, where my cousin Ahmed and good friend Jacob Roca would accompany on my walk to the ring holding my IBO and IBF World Titles high and proud. I chose to walk to the ring to the sound of Rhianna and T.I.'s hit track 'Live Your Life'. The words to this song saying exactly how I felt in that moment.

I was the current IBF Featherweight Champion of the World; my life couldn't be any better. I was living out my childhood dreams and I truly felt I was destined for boxing superstardom. But I had to remember to live in the moment and be grateful for what I had.

The bout with Juan was an absolute tear up. His southpaw style was a hard code to crack, but I chipped away at him, round after round. A lot of drama unfolded during the course of the bout and even though I was in total control, I was being made to work extremely hard to secure the win. Juan was a genuine threat and I was super glad I didn't take him lightly. Midway through the bout Billy Hussein lit a match under my butt when he asked me to show him I was ready to defend my crown against the likes of Gary Russell Jr. My brother and manager, Emaid, also made his way to the corner, urging me to win as he had some major news for me.

With just two rounds left in the bout, I suffered a nasty gash to my left eye, courtesy of an intentional headbutt from Juan, who was becoming desperate as he was way behind on the scorecards.

Going into the last round, Billy instructed me to box cautiously to ensure the victory, but my warrior instinct told me knock Juan out. I wanted to continue my knockout streak, so I chased him down looking to close the show, only to be headbutted intentionally once again, causing a major cut, this time on my right eye. I was a bloody mess. The fight had turned into a bar room brawl ending with Juan and me going toe-to-toe until the final bell. Once the final bell was rung, I was relieved the war was over and I knew I had secured another entertaining victory.

We went to the scorecards which read 97-94, 98-92, 99-92 and once again, I was declared the victor by a unanimous decision. I later learnt the bout with Juan was voted as one of the best fights of 2012.

As soon as I made my way to the change room, I asked my brother what the good news was, his response was quick, 'Never mind, we'll talk about it once you've soaked up this win and come back from your holiday in Dubai.' I was off; ten days in the Middle East with the Prince, my brother and Naseem Hamed. After only being in Dubai for seven days, I received a phone call from Emaid asking if I could meet him in Las Vegas. He explained Floyd Mayweather had joined forces with 50 Cent and had set up a promotional company called TMT Promotions. They had expressed their intentions in signing me to the company. I decided to fly back to Australia in order to regroup with my team and set up the trip to Las Vegas.

Arriving back in Sydney, Emaid mentioned he had spoken to 50 Cent and our travel arrangements have been made. We would only meet with 50 Cent as Floyd Mayweather had been incarcerated due to a domestic violence charge.

Emaid explained 50 Cent had been given instructions by Floyd to put the deal together. On 27 July 2012, we travelled business class to the USA courtesy of TMT Promotions. The excitement was real. During the flight, millions of scenarios crossed my mind; how would this all go down? The thought of being signed to a company owned by Floyd Mayweather and 50 Cent was mind-blowing.

I was reminded of many years earlier when I had fought on the undercard of Mayweather vs. De La Hoyer. After the fight, while waiting outside Oscar's change room, Floyd had stopped to greet me, applauding me for my victory and performance.

When we arrived in Las Vegas, 50 Cent's driver, Tommy Smalls, picked us up and drove us to the M Hotel. He notified us 50 would come through to pick us up later on. I was very tired, so I decided to take a nap. A few hours later, Emaid woke me to tell me to get ready, as 50 was on his way.

After getting ready, we headed to the lobby where we met with my advisor, Mike Altamura, to discuss our approach on how to deal with this offer. Emaid reminded me to stay cool and be professional. Minutes later, a Lamborghini, Rolls-Royce and a Bentley parked up at the front of the M Hotel.

50 Cent stepped out of the Lamborghini and headed towards us. I stayed cool taking my brother's advice, and 50 was kind enough to take plenty of photos with us.

Before we headed off to dinner, I asked 50 if he had remembered who I was. He quickly responded, reminding me of the night Floyd had beaten Oscar. 50 and I jumped into the 'lambo' and cranked his tunes. The feeling was surreal. Here I was, a young man, born and bred in Sydney, hanging out with one of the world's leading rap stars.

When we arrived at the Hard Rock Hotel, 50 and I, alongside Emaid and Mike walked towards a Chinese restaurant. Fans were stopping 50, losing their minds, many of them mistaking me for a rap star by the name of Drake. 'No this is not Drake,' 50 would tell them, 'this is the IBF Champ of the World, Billy Dibbs.'

While sitting in the restaurant, 50 made many calls to boxing sites letting them know I was the latest signing to the TMT team. I wasn't too happy about this, as my brother was in negotiations with Golden Boy Promotions about a possible showdown with Gary Russell Jr. They had formally made an offer of $350,000; an offer 50 Cent deemed as 'chump change for a champion'.

To me, it seemed as though 50 was jumping the gun. How could he be so sure I would be happy with their offer and sign on? He mentioned they had already signed Gamboa and Andre Dirrell to the TMT banner, and I would be as happy as they both were.

After leaving the restaurant, we got back in the cars and 50 had organised a night out. Arriving at the location, something didn't sit right. The place looked like a factory, and there were plenty of amazing cars. As we entered the building, 50 had a few bricks of money with him, but I still had no idea what we were about to walk into. I couldn't believe it when we walked into a strip club. Emaid and I were extremely uncomfortable, for many reasons. The number-one reason being that it was the month of Ramadan. Emaid looked at me and said, 'We need to get out of here.' I agreed and told 50 we were not comfortable and were going to leave. I explained to him it was Ramadan and places like this were forbidden to Muslims. To my surprise, 50 decided to leave with us.

As we walked out a young lady called out, 'Hey, 50 … where are you going?'

His response had us in stitches: 'Baby, you lucky it's Ramadan.'

The following morning, my brother received an email from Eric Gomez notifying him Gary Russell Jr was not interested in the fight. This now halted our negotiations with GBP and we were full steam into locking down a great deal with TMT Promotions. About the fight with Russell, a journalist by the name of Nick Walshaw was forced to apologise in a newspaper article after falsely accusing me of ducking Russell Jr and being afraid of the match up. When we showed him the correspondence, he was left swallowing his words. This bought me much satisfaction.

On the evening of the 28th, a driver picked up Emaid, Mike and me to meet with 50. So many thoughts were running through my mind as we sat with 50 and Tommy Smalls. The moment of truth had finally arrived. After back-and-forth discussions, 50 finally made an offer that was hard to refuse.

He presented a three-year, nine-fight package estimated at a minimum of US$2 million. Before agreeing to anything, Emaid and Mike contacted Adam Houda to discuss the offer. Once Adam had reviewed it, we agreed to sign on. The deal was done and 50 got directly on the phone, notifying numerous media outlets about the news, including a live conversation with Fox Sports Australia. This was all so exciting. I had finally made it to the big time. After years of grinding away in Australia, I was about to get my second opportunity to showcase my skills in the US. I would no longer have to fight in obscure venues and now had the chance to get guaranteed money without the responsibility of promoting our own shows. I was finally considered hot property.

To top this amazing night off, 50 Cent asked me to follow him outside. He walked towards his Rolls-Royce, opened the trunk and grabbed a backpack, tipping it upside-down. 'Welcome to the money team, champ. This is a little bonus for you,' he said as he threw me some cash. I was shocked; the night couldn't get any better. We posed for a few photos showing off the cash, than headed back inside.

I told my brother about what had transpired and he reminded me to, 'Stay cool, we'll discuss this later!'

By this time, it was well past midnight and 50 drove us back to our hotel. Emaid and I stayed up to the wee hours of the morning talking about what had happened; it was truly mind-blowing. After spending the next few days in Vegas, soaking it all in, we flew back to Australia. My life really had changed. It was so cool; I could pick up the phone at any time and call 50. One night while hanging out with my cousin Ahmed and some friends, I contacted 50 and put my cousin, Ahmed, on the phone to chat with him. This was something that didn't happen to a kid from Australia; it almost felt too good to be true.

A few weeks after signing this life-changing contract, I went car shopping. My brother Emaid was not only my manager, he was also rated the number-one salesman in Australia for BMW, and he organised one of his colleagues to help me. They allowed me to test-drive a BMW 335 Individual. It was a very unique colour, one you wouldn't usually see, so I wanted it. They allowed me to take the car for a few days to test it, so I could take my time in making a decision.

I felt so proud; after all these years of hard work, I could finally see it paying off. This was how I envisioned life would be as champion of the world.

A few days after picking up the BMW, I decided to go for a late-night ride on my own. At approximately 9pm, I was driving home through Mortdale, when I noticed a dark silver BMW with no number plates following me. During this time, I was on the phone with Adam Houda discussing my contract with TMT Promotions. I mentioned to Adam I felt I was being followed. He told me to remain cool and continue my journey home. I stepped up my speed to try and lose the car following me, but they stayed right on my tail. I just couldn't lose them. Driving on Belmore Road, I was passing through the area of Riverwood, when I got caught at a set of lights. Looking through the rear-view mirror, I noticed the driver had dimmed their lights before pulling up slowly on my left-hand side. What transpired next would send me into a frantic shock. This driver pointed a gun out of his window, aiming it directly at me. I stepped as hard as I could on the pedal while screaming to Adam that this person had a gun. He instructed me to go as quickly as possible to Bankstown Police Station. While speeding towards Canterbury Road, I ran a few red lights, but the driver wouldn't give up and continued to follow me. As I approached Canterbury Road, I saw a truck coming and took my chances, running the red light, only just missing the oncoming truck and losing the driver who was following me in the process.

As I arrived at Bankstown Police Station, I heard three police cars, their sirens blaring as they boxed me in. A police officer would then draw his gun, whilst screaming at me to get out of the car. Adam was still on the line and screamed through the car speakers that I was the one being pursued. At this point, the police officers instructed me to get home, saying they would contact me the following day to go through what exactly had happened, as they could clearly see how shaken up I was. I was in complete shock, shaking so frantically I could barely dial Emaid's number. I explained to him what had happened, and he made his way to Bankstown Police Station as quickly as he could. We swapped cars and I made my way home.

Over the next few days, I could not believe what had transpired that night. Was somebody out to get me? Could it have been a mistaken identity? After doing a background search on the car, the police worked out the car I had just picked up from the BMW dealership was traded in by a known drug dealer. I had been in the wrong place at the wrong time and had 'nothing to worry about'. Still, I took no chances and was quick to rid myself of the car.

On 5 November 2012 – yes, a few months after I'd signed with TMT – a famed boxing journalist by the name of Dan Rafael wrote an article. *50 Cent and Floyd Mayweather are DONE.*

Weeks before this article dropped, I received a call from Sekou Gary, a US attorney who was working on behalf of 50 Cent. He told me both 50 and Floyd would no longer be working together and I would need to decide the direction I would take moving forward. I was baffled and shocked to hear this news, so I contacted Floyd and Leonard Ellerbe to try and work out what happened.

Floyd suggested I give 50 back the bonus money and cut my ties with him, claiming he would re-sign me to a new contract, as he was 'not very pleased' with the agreement that had been drawn up by 50's legal team.

After a discussion with Floyd, I contacted 50, who told me he and Floyd had fallen out over a few issues. He explained he had great ideas and big plans to collaborate both boxing and music in cross-over promotions, merging both crowds. He said Floyd was only concerned about his career and if I wanted out of the contract, I would need to return the bonus money he gave me. I then contacted Floyd asking him if he could help by giving 50 back the bonus money. Still, he declined, saying I should give everything back and then he would renegotiate my contract with my team and me. 50 was to form a new company called SMS Promotions. Both Dirrell and Gamboa had made the choice to stick with 50, so I followed suit. This decision would be one I would regret, but I'll come back to that.

CHAPTER THIRTEEN
SMS PROMOTIONS JOURNEY

N ow officially signed to 50 Cent's SMS Promotions, I was set to make my return to the ring on American soil. My bout would serve as the chief support to future hall-of-famer, Miguel Cotto, who would be facing off against a champion in his own right, Austin Trout. The date was set: 1 December. The venue: Madison Square Garden. This was to be the second time I would appear at this historic venue, the last being in a sensational victory against Rogers Mtagwa on the undercard of Mosley vs. Cotto. This time I would face undefeated Puerto Rican Jayson Velez, who was promoted by boxing powerhouse Golden Boy Promotions. He boasted an impressive 19-0 record with fourteen remarkable victories. The camp was underway. Billy decided we would head to the Gold Coast for some world-class sparring with former Olympian and world champion, Michael Katsidis. To make things even better, one of my favourite humans and lawyer, Adam Houda, would accompany us. After a few good days of solid training and sparring, I decided to get an early night's sleep. Upon waking up the next morning, I looked at my phone only to be shocked with what I saw. *Billy Dib no longer chief support to Cotto vs. Trout.* It seemed I was the victim of 50 Cent and Floyd Mayweather's crossfire. Showtime had struck a deal with Floyd who was advised by Al Haymon, who had a stake in this promotion. It all made sense. Why would they help a 50 Cent fighter?

My choice to work with 50 was already proving to be a wrong move. After seeing the tweets and reading the boxing news, I walked into the lounge room to break the news to Billy and Adam. They already knew of the ill-fated information. After a short discussion, Adam contacted 50 Cent to discuss what had transpired. 50 assured Adam not to worry. He would get me on another show, or he would promote one. I was very disappointed. This would have been a great platform to showcase my skills on a prime-time network in the United States.

It was back to the drawing board for me. I decided to take a little holiday to Thailand to recharge my batteries. My younger brother Youssef and cousin Reyad would accompany me. After a great holiday where we randomly ran into Hollywood action hero Jean Claude Van Damme, it was back to Sydney to start training again. The IBF had decided I would now face the mandatory challenger, Mauricio Javier Munoz who had defeated Cuban contender Luis Franco in an official IBF Eliminator. Just as the camp was about to start, Munoz withdrew from the bout. The IBF mandated Luis would be next in line. The date was set for 1 March 2013. The venue was to be Foxwoods Resort Casino in Mashantucket, where my childhood hero Naseem Hamed had famously brutally stretched Augie Sanchez.

Less than a month before Franco and I would face-off, disaster would strike once again. Franco abruptly withdrew from the bout. I was furious. I had been on the shelf for seven frustrating months. Franco released a statement outlining he would not face me in a world title bout for a measly $20,000. I couldn't blame him, as that was considered terrible money for a world title bout.

After getting caught up in legal issues, Franco claimed he would retire from the sport of boxing. Once again, I was left without an opponent. How could this be happening to me? I felt so degraded. I was the IBF Champion of the World, but I wasn't fighting.

Less than a month until the ESPN televised date, we were left scrambling for a replacement opponent. Many contenders were offered the opportunity, but still, they turned it down. The fight was offered to LA-based Russian Evgeny Gradovich, who initially turned it down, but would change his mind after his trainer, Robert Garcia, advised him otherwise. Robert and I had a history, as he had trained Steven Luevano who put a sole loss on my boxing résumé back in 2008.

With less than four weeks until the bout, I needed to get to work. In the months leading to the bout, I had prepared for Jayson Velez, Munoz, Franco and now, finally, Gradovich.

CHAPTER FOURTEEN
GRADOVICH

With the bout with Gradovich formally announced, training was in full swing. One evening after a workout, I could feel my throat getting sore. I took some medication, but it didn't help as days passed. I tried to train through the pain only to end up bedridden for days. After a visit to my family doctor, Jamal Rifi, he indicated I had a throat infection and should withdraw from the bout. How could I do that? I had already been out of the ring for seven months and the bills were piling up.

I decided to fight despite Dr Jamal's wishes. On 20 February, I, Billy Hussein, Adam Houda, my brother Youssef and a few team members boarded a flight to LA to wrap up camp before heading to Connecticut where the fight would take place – live on ESPN. During my time in LA, I would wrap up my sparring with Oscar Valdez, a former Olympian and future world champion. The sparring went exceptionally well even though I was still getting over my throat infection.

After a short five-day stint in LA, it was time for the team and me to head New York, with only five days left until the bout with Gradovich. Upon arriving in NY I got a surprise that would put on a major high. My cousins, Ahmed 'baby face' and Shereef, would make the trip to NY to be with me before heading to Connecticut. It would have been the first time in a long stint I would fight without my cousin Ahmed by my side. Three days before our world championship bout, a press conference would take place. It was here, for the first time, I would see and face-off against Gradovich. After an eventful press conference my team and I boarded a van; it was the final leg of our trip heading to Connecticut. With the weigh-in two days away, I didn't have much weight to cut. This was due to me being sick and not having much of an appetite. It helped, as I could be in cruise control going into the weigh-in. The official weigh-in took place on 28 February. Gradovich was first to grace the scales, coming in precisely on the 57.15kg limit. I then got on the scales and came in at an even 57kg. I had a gang of fans with me, as well as my corner team Billy Hussein and Hussein Hussein, who was a former Olympian and elite fly contender weight, who challenged for world title honours on a few occasions, just coming up short. My corner would also consist of Brian Wilmott, my cutman, and my brother Mohammed, who had been working my corner since day one.

After refuelling, the team and I, as well as our Aussie contingent, decided to head out for an early night at the movies. The atmosphere was quite relaxed, though with a crew close to twenty you can always bet some fun is going to take place. As we headed to the movies, the boys pulled over to have a snow fight. My eldest brother Jihad, who was somewhat of a father-figure, wouldn't let me out of the van as I was getting over being sick and couldn't afford to get hit by some stray snow.

As 1 March finally arrived, for some bizarre reason I had a terrible night's sleep. I tossed and turned all night and wasn't feeling myself. Was it a case of nerves getting the better of me? Or was it my preparations for so many different opponents? Or perhaps it was the fact that less than two weeks ago I was bedridden with a terrible throat infection. I don't know, but I started questioning myself. Hours before heading to the venue, my brother Youssef and teammate Billel Dib visited me in my room. I told them how I was feeling and they tried to calm me down telling me it was nerves; I would be okay once we touched gloves and the bell was rung. But that was far from the truth. A part of me felt I needed my mother, as had happened in the past. She was the only one who could calm me.

Upon leaving my room, we headed to the venue and I asked all those accompanying me to walk ahead as I wanted to share a private conversation with my mother. The truth was, I didn't want them to see me cry. I called Mum and asked her not to watch the fight as it would be shown across the world live on ESPN. 'Why?' she responded; I broke down telling her I wasn't feeling myself. She told me to believe in myself: 'You are champion for a reason.'

As I got to the change room, I wiped my tears and pulled myself together. My corner, my brothers, my cousin Ahmed and Adam surrounded me as I warmed up for my battle with Evgeny Gradovich. It was time to make my ring walk accompanied by my brothers and Adam. 50 would walk us to the ring rapping his latest hit, 'New Day'. It was quite fitting, as my last US appearance was entirely lacklustre. My time to shine on the big stage had finally arrived. It was time for me to show the world that the Billy Dib who boxed Steven Luevano in a lacklustre effort back in 2008 was no longer. I was the new-and-improved version. It was supposed to be a new day.

Sadly, it wasn't to be. Even though I started the bout well, winning the first five rounds on all judges' cards, Gradovich rallied back after I suffered a severe gash to the back of my head, caused by an accidental elbow from Gradovich that would later require four staples. The blood wouldn't end there as the fight slowly shifted into an all-out war. Many headbutts would come into play, turning the battle into a bloodbath. Both Gradovich and I were looking worse for wear. In round eight of the hotly contested bout, referee Eddie Claudio would strip me of a point for holding. This would prove very detrimental at the end of the bout. The closing rounds were total war. Both of my eyebrows were leaking blood and I had two gashes to my head; it was only adrenalin that would get me to the final bell.

When the final bell rung, 50 Cent, Lou Dibella the co-promoter, as well as matchmaker Sean Gibbons, all got in the ring and told me I surely had pulled out the win.

Standing centre ring, looking worse for wear after suffering multiple lacerations that would require a total of seven staples and over twenty stitches, we went to the scorecards.

Referee Don Trella sees it 114-112 Gradovich.

Referee Don Ackerman has it 114-112 Dib.

And Glenn Feldman has it 114-112.

For your winner AND THE NEW CHAMPION OF THE WORLD – EVGANY 'THE MEXICAN RUSSIAN' GRADOVICH.

I was heartbroken. The title I had worked so hard to attain had slipped away. I leaned over and placed my head on Jihad's shoulder; the tears began to flow. 'Keep your chin up; we are all so proud of you.'

Lou Dibella added, 'No shame in that performance, your stocks have risen.'

One thing was for sure: the memory of my lacklustre performance back in 2008 had been erased.

Back in the change room, reality set in. I was in tears. I decided to lay down, only for the paramedics to come in asking, 'Why are you laying down?' They pleaded with me to get onto the stretcher as they wanted to take me to the hospital for a check-up. I refused. 50 Cent and Lou Dibella became agitated with me and forced me onto the stretcher. In that exact moment, I began to vomit violently. I was rushed to Connecticut Hospital, and from then, the night was a blur.

I do remember one thing: a nurse asking me to rate my pain from 1-10. My response was, 'Ten.' I actually felt as though my brain was going to explode. My family and cousins were overly concerned when I asked them to play the Quran. I thought I was going to die.

The following morning, a nurse woke me, offering some juice. I fell right back to sleep, only to wake up in the afternoon in my hotel room. *How did I get here?* I wondered. I looked around the room at my family lying around on the hotel floor. I couldn't work out what had happened. I saw my IBF World Title resting on the table. My initial thought was, *Oh my God, I won! It's all been a bad dream.* But after looking at my phone, I realised this was no dream and I had lost. I rushed to the bathroom. My face was a mess. It looked like I had been assaulted with a bat.

I began to weep. I heard a knock on the door; it was my brother. He had listened to my cries. He hugged me, saying, 'Stay calm. Everything is going to be okay. There is more to life than boxing. You have already accomplished so much.'

I looked him right in the face and said, 'We have a rematch clause, and I want to exercise it.'

He laughed and said, 'What happened to retiring?' Apparently, at the hospital, I was telling everyone I was done with the sport.

As the rest of the team were waking up, I couldn't help it; I started to cry again. My cousins, Sherriff and Ahmed, tried their best to ease my pain.

Everyone around me pleaded with me not to worry: 'WE WILL GET IT BACK.'

The next morning, we headed to New York as a team. Emaid had organised to meet with 50 Cent before we left for Australia.

As 50 Cent approached me he said, 'Champ, don't worry. It was a great fight. The networks were very impressed. We will set up the rematch, and you will be champion again soon.'

That evening we boarded a flight back home to Sydney. I kept to myself and cried the whole way home. A Qantas member by the name of Justin Rumour made an announcement over the intercom congratulating me on a 'warrior-like' performance and wished me the best in recapturing the IBF crown. Everyone onboard began applauding me.

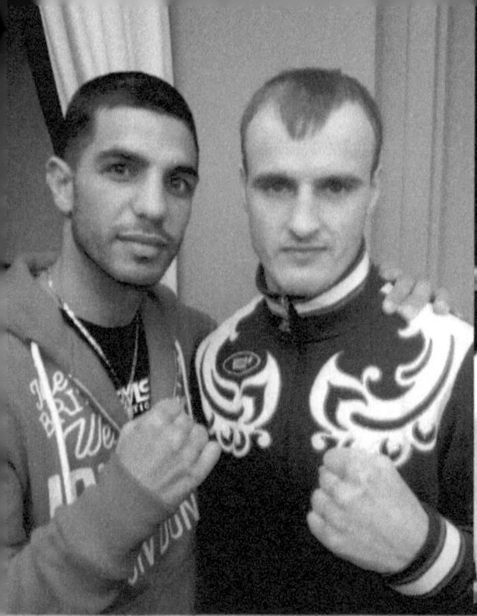

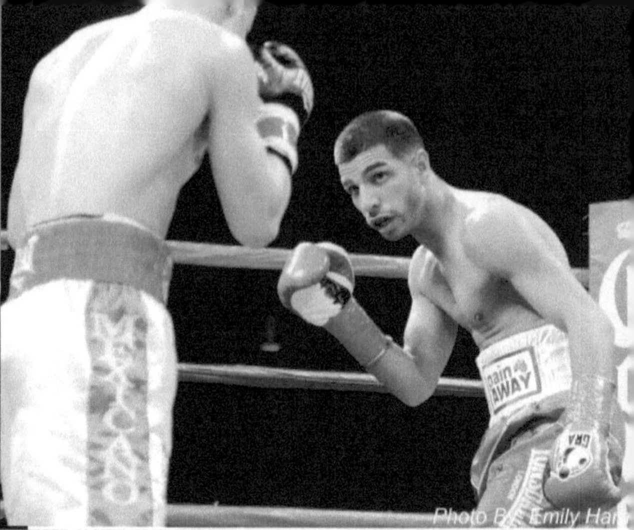

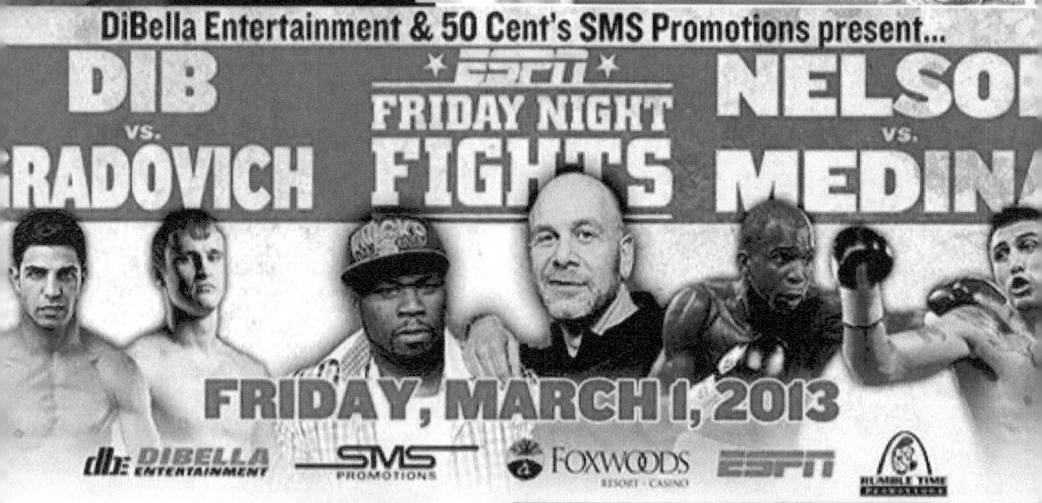

DiBella Entertainment & 50 Cent's SMS Promotions present...

DIB vs. GRADOVICH — ESPN FRIDAY NIGHT FIGHTS — NELSON vs. MEDINA

FRIDAY, MARCH 1, 2013

 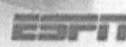

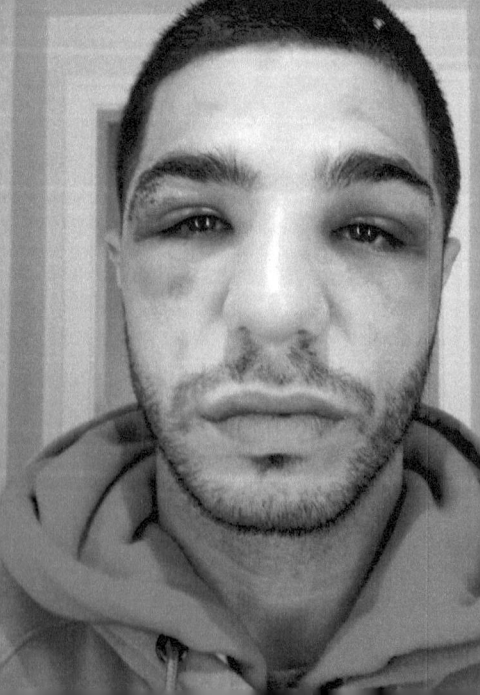

CHAPTER FIFTEEN
THE REMATCH

Back to the drawing board; it was a few weeks before I learnt the IBF would allow Gradovich to have a voluntary defence before facing me in a much-anticipated rematch. His opponent would be Mauricio Munoz, a man I was set to meet before he pulled out with an injury.

Next up for me was a ten-round televised bout in the state of Connecticut against upset-minded Mike Oliver, a Connecticut resident who boasted a record of twenty-five victories with only three defeats.

As a team, Billy Hussein and I looked to make some adjustments. We added NBL star James Harvey to the team, bringing a whole new element. James and I had developed a close relationship over the past few years, so having him in the camp was a significant buzz. I decided to start camp with James in Queensland before heading back to Sydney to knuckle down before heading to NY to wrap up. I was determined to get back in the winning circle, setting up my rematch with Evgeny for the IBF crown.

We headed to NY two weeks before the bout would take place, making sure I was 100% acclimatised. The camp was smooth sailing as the team at SMS made sure everything was on point. I had developed a close relationship with 50 Cent's employees, Monique Myers being one of them. She made sure everything ran smoothly and we were all looked after.

This time around, things were a little different than my regular team. Emaid, Jihad, as well Mohammed and Adam couldn't be there to support me on my journey back.

Making weight was no issue. On 4 July I weighed in at 127lb (57.6kg), just one pound over the featherweight limit of 126. When the stare-down took place, Mike decided to go a step too far by placing his forehead on mine; instinctively I grabbed him around the throat. 50 Cent pulled us apart. The stage was set. I knew I wanted to hurt this man.

The bout with Oliver was nothing less than horrible. He was a very awkward customer who was looking for an easy way out, complaining at every possible chance he got. Even though I won a comfortable decision, it wasn't one of my better performances. The scores after the bout were 96-92, 96-92 and 94-94. I made the necessary adjustments to secure the victory.

Coming into the bout, I felt the weight of the world on my shoulders, so once the decision was read that I was victorious, I could now focus on the rematch against Gradovich. I felt having James onboard helped to freshen up my approach. After a successful result, I headed home to soak up the victory and spend time with my family and friends. It was now a waiting game. Gradovich was set to face Munoz twenty-two days after I met Oliver. The rematch would only take place if Gradovich was successful in defending his title – which he was!

The stage was set at the Venetian Resort in Macao, China for 24 November 2013. The rematch would land on a huge card headlined by the legendary Manny Pacquiao vs. Brandon Rios. Televised by heavyweight network HBO, this was my chance to make a statement after being blacklisted by HBO for many years. The first encounter between Gradovich and me was so exciting, HBO didn't want to pass up on the opportunity to telecast a cracking rematch.

With the rematch set, it was now time to start camp. Unfortunately, James was not able to join us for this camp due to work commitments, so Billy and Adam decided to bring in former Commonwealth and Olympian representative, John Steffensen. He enjoyed great success in winning Commonwealth Gold in 2006, as well as a silver medal at the 2004 Olympic Games.

Camp commenced on 1 October, giving me just over eight weeks to prepare for my much-anticipated rematch. Evgany was a very good pressure fighter, so we worked closely with Dylan Emery and Tony Bates, as they were both high-volume punchers.

Many things changed for this camp as the fight was in China and would be televised live on HBO, meaning Gradovich and I would be fighting at approximately 9am China time, which was 6am Sydney time. This was definitely not going to be an easy task. To accommodate these times, Billy adjusted my training to 6am every morning. We also implemented many running drills to build my engine, as we knew Gradovich would bring a solid pace throughout the bout.

After seven solid weeks, my team and I boarded a flight to Macau with the intention of bringing the IBF crown back home. Everything was on point. Training camp was enjoyable, and it showed as my weight was on point.

A few days after arriving in China, the atmosphere began to build as the HBO crew and other fighters began to arrive. 50 Cent's promotional team, including Monique Myers, were my representatives as 50 Cent couldn't be present. At the HBO fighter meeting, I spoke with the great Roy Jones Jr, as well as Jim Lampley and Larry Merchant who were working as the commentary team.

I explained my first encounter with Gradovich saw many things go in his favour, and I felt the rematch would be better. On the morning of the 23rd, I woke up weighing 57.4kg – 300g over the featherweight limit of 57.1kg.

After spending close to five minutes in a hot bath, I wrapped myself in a few towels and lay under my blanket. Ten minutes later, I showered and jumped on the scales weighing exactly 57.1kg. The team and I made our way to the weigh-in, that was open to the public.

The atmosphere was terrific. I was so proud to be the main supporting bout to Pac Man vs. Rios. I would appear on a massive stage, televised by HBO PPV. It doesn't get any better than that.

I was called to the scale, coming in .05kg over the limit! I was shocked; my team scrambled to get a towel as I was forced to get back on the scales in the nude. I was so embarrassed, nevertheless, I made the weight and the rematch was in play.

During the stare-down, Gradovich's eyes looked as cold as ice. I smiled at him and left the stage. Now to replenish – this job was left to John. The fight was interesting in so many ways. Being the fact Gradovich and I would meet in the early hours of the morning meaning the mandatory second-day weigh-in would be at 8pm the same day as the official weigh-in. We were both successful in coming in under the 10% weight gain limit.

As I lay in bed that night, I envisioned being announced as the new champion of the world. I was happy to be sharing a room with Emaid who had steered the majority of my career. We chatted for hours talking about the journey of my career and how we worked so hard to get back here. I fell asleep around 11pm only to be woken by John at 5:45am as I needed to have an early meal before facing Gradovich at 9am.

Moments before heading to the venue, my family and friends gathered in my room as Adam had called for them to join us. Adam delivered a spine-chilling speech which left many of us with tears in our eyes. Adam spoke of the days of our Prophets and how they would choose a soldier to lead them into battle. He explained I was 'the chosen one'. He also mentioned they were all proud of me – win, lose or draw. It was genuinely touching.

After Adam's beautiful words, I hugged and thanked each individual who made his way support me. Arriving at the change room at 7:30am, we had a little under two hours until fight time. John helped run me through my stretches as I tried to wake my body up. I was slowly getting into my boxing attire and it was time for Brian to wrap my hands in front of the official commission.

Shortly after gloving up, I felt the urge to use the restroom. My cousin Reyad was left with the honours of helping me! I was back in the change room when Robert Garcia walked in demanding I take my gloves off so he could examine my hand wraps. I explained to him that the commissioner had watched me tape my hands and glove up.

He still demanded I take them off. After a back-and-forth argument, I complied with his request. Adam and a few of the other team members kept saying, 'Don't worry, Billy, he's just scared, don't let it bother you.' I knew Robert was trying to play mind games.

After being re-gloved, it was back to business. I did some pad work before the team gathered around as my father gave a final prayer. I made my way to the ring, followed by Gradovich. The particulars are read by no other than Michael Buffer. His famous words ring around the arena: 'LET'S GET READY TO RUMBLE.'

Gradovich and I touch gloves and head back to our respected corners. DING, DING – the fight is on.

Billy instructed me to win the first round at all costs. In typical Gradovich style, he came out being very rough and messy. The first round is always testing as both of us try to establish our plan. One thing I remember even after winning the first round was how hard Gradovich was hitting. It seemed as though his punches were ten times stronger than our first fight. I told Billy and his brother Hussein I felt as though his gloves were loaded.

Winning the first round on all judges' cards, the bout turned into a back-and-forth battle between rounds one to five. Things began to spiral downhill in round six after I suffered a flash knockdown. I had now been officially knocked down three times in my career. The championship was slipping away, but there was no quit in me.

After the completion of round eight, Billy spoke with much urgency telling me my father had signalled for him to stop the fight. 'Disregard what my father is saying, tell him to leave the arena.'

Billy asked me to show him some vintage Billy Dib in round nine, or he would be forced to pull the pin. After getting clipped with a few good shots, Billy stepped up onto the ring apron calling for the ref to stop the fight. I couldn't believe it, I pleaded with him. 'Why did you do that?' For the first time in my career, I had been stopped. Not by a fighter but by my trainer who felt he had seen enough. Completely deflated and emotionally broken, I congratulated Gradovich and his team before making my way back to the change room.

It was at this point I felt some foul play. A supervisor handed me a urine cup telling me to give it back to him 'once I'm ready'. I couldn't believe it. I passed the cup to my brother Mohammed and told him to pee in it, as there was no supervisor to watch for foul play. My father was infuriated. He demanded both Gradovich and I do the urine sample in front of each other, but Gradovich's team declined.

A big part of me felt as though Gradovich was geared up, but I would never know as no 'real' urine sample was taken. I calmed myself and prayed. I had faith the Almighty had better plans for me. I let it go and prepared myself mentally to move on.

After getting showered up, I headed to the press conference where many media outlets met me. Bob Arum introduced me to the stage to share my thoughts on the outcome of the bout and my performance.

I thanked Evgeny and his team for the opportunity, as well as the HBO networks whom were very impressed with my performance. I explained I was grateful for the chance, thanking my team, brother Emaid, as well as the team at SMS and Monique Myers.

'Two men showcased their abilities today, but only one man can be victorious, and today that was Evgeny. I have no excuses. God has others plans for me. I'll be back.'

CHAPTER SIXTEEN
NEXT STEPS

Back to the drawing board it was – again. I had officially suffered my third career defeat. I took some time away from the sport of boxing, concentrating on life outside of the gym and ring.

The months following my third defeat were quite difficult; failing to regain my featherweight crown had me second-guessing myself. The fact being that I'd been a fighter throughout my whole life, I felt lost. What direction would I take? What would happen to my SMS contract? I was battling inner demons. Boxing was the only thing I knew. I was single with a lot of time on my hands. My luck was set to change when a relative of mine contacted me asking if I was still single. I immediately responded with a smile on my face saying, 'Yes, why do you ask?'

Hayatt went on to explain how she had found my perfect match, and it was a girl I was familiar with. I smiled from ear to ear, 'Don't you think if I knew her I wouldn't have approached the situation.'

They say no man is complete until he finds the one who completes him. Here's where it all starts. I had met Sara back when she was at school and her mother Gada approached me asking if I could help her with a school assignment based on positive role models. Of course, I was happy to help.

'Hayatt, Sara is about thirteen years of age,' I laughed.

'No, she is now nineteen and stunning,' she said.

I explained to Hayatt that I wasn't sure Sara would be interested in a man who was eight years her senior. Her response suggested otherwise as though she knew something I didn't: 'You'd be surprised.'

Following my chat with Hayatt, I reached out to Sara through Facebook asking her if there was any truth in what Hayatt was saying. She indicated there might be some interest though she was very cagey. Still, I got the feeling she was interested in me.

While this was going on, Billy Hussein was mapping out my comeback and the third phase of my career. Back to super featherweight where I had previously captured the IBO super featherweight crown. Life was back on track. After the dark, I could now finally see the light.

The plan was to step up in weight in a bid to capture my third world title. After seven months away from the sport of boxing I was set to make my long-awaited return. This time, it would be in a ten-round bout, live on ESPN, against well-credentialed Alberto Garza. The bout was set to take place on 2 July 2014 back at Foxwoods Resort Casino, where it all went wrong back on a cold night in 2013 against Evgeny Gradovich.

Garza was a former silver WBC champion and a WBA world title challenger, so this would be no easy task, and I was coming off a devastating ninth-round TKO loss.

I was in a really good place, having met my potential future wife months earlier. The saying goes, 'A good fighter is a dangerous fighter.' I was feeling thrilled at the chance to resurrect my career for the third time as well as finding love along the way.

With all this being said, I wasn't looking forward to being away from my future wife, Sara Selim.

Let me rewind this a little. After confirming Sara's potential feelings, I asked if she would be interested in possibly catching up for a coffee and a chat. Her response word for word was, 'Yeah, sounds good, but it might need to be when I come back from Thailand.' I asked Sara if her parents would be upset if they found out I was trying to connect with her.

Sara's response was very promising, 'God, no. My parents love your family as much as I do.' With that response, I was 100% convinced that what Hayatt had been telling me was true. Sara and I exchanged numbers, but before I would call her, I decided to reach out to Sara's father, Ibby. I told Sara of my intentions; she was pleased to hear this, as she shared an excellent relationship with her dad.

I remember the phone call as though it was yesterday. I was so nervous, but I summoned up the confidence to make the call. I had never done this before, it was as almost as though I was stepping into the ring. Sara's father was a travel agent who had booked me a few flights in the past, so when I rang him, his first impression was I was calling to book a flight.

'I'm not calling about a flight, Uncle Ibby.' Embarrassed, I managed to blab it out, 'I'm interested in getting to know your daughter Sara.'

His response shocked me. 'Wow, are you serious? That's wonderful news, we love your family.' I explained I had chatted with Sara on Facebook and wanted to do the right thing and come through the front door, as a man should.

Ibby invited me to share some lunch with the family the next day, but I explained to him that Sara felt it was best I come over once they had returned from Thailand. Ibby was adamant I visit before they left.

I contacted Sara and relayed the terrific outcome of my call. She was pleased, yet very surprised her father had invited me over.

The following day I woke up with butterflies; nervous yet so excited. I contacted my cousin Hayatt and asked if she would accompany me the next morning as I was super nervous and didn't feel I could do it on my own.

D-day – on my way to pick up my cousin, I couldn't believe my luck had turned so much; I was potentially driving to meet with my future. I picked up Hayatt, stopping at a patisserie before making our way to Sara's home. With my heart pounding, we eventually arrived in Cronulla, where Sara lived with her mother, father and siblings. I rang the doorbell. Ibby greeted us and welcomed us in. Sara's mother, Gada, was delighted to see me and was super excited about the possibility of Sara and me.

I wondered where Sara was, only to hear her footsteps as she made her way down the stairs towards us. Wow, she was beautiful. So natural. Wearing no shoes, a baggy T-shirt and a pair of shorts, she was what I was searching for. I remember time passing by so fast. I was having a wonderful time as Sara's parents helped to ease the mood so I was as comfortable as could be. Being mindful not to overstay my welcome, I tried to leave on a few occasions, only to have Sara's parents stop me.

After a few tries, Hayatt and I finally picked ourselves up and said our goodbyes before heading off. Driving home, I couldn't wipe the smile off my face. I had potentially met the one who would complete me; she was cute, funny and full of character. A part of me was a little sad thinking Sara and her family would leave for Thailand in less than a week. Upon arriving home, I spoke to my mother and father with so much excitement, I had a real kick in my step. They were happy to hear this excellent news. My father contacted Ibby to thank him for being very hospitable. Ibby asked my father to visit before they left for Thailand. I was so happy to hear I would get another chance to see Sara before she left for two weeks.

The day before Sara's family left for Thailand, we visited along with my Aunty Hoda and Uncle Husam. Time always seemed to pass by so fast. I wish I could have paused time as I was so happy to be in the presence of this beautiful soul. Before leaving, my father and Ibby decided that upon their return from Thailand, we would make our intentions clear by performing the Fatiha in the presence of our loved ones.

With Sara and her family now holidaying in one of Sara's favourite locations, Phuket, I was back on the grind, preparing for my next challenge. Life was on the up; Sara had a positive effect on my life.

After two long weeks, Sara and her family were back; I hadn't been so excited in many years. We had so much to prepare. Everything was following so smoothly. It was as though Sara knew her time in this world was limited with so much yet to achieve before she would depart this world.

One of my happiest days was 27 April 2014; everything in life seemed so perfect. For years I had been married to the sport of boxing with no direction in regard to my love life. I had finally found what every man yearns for: true love. Before this godsend, I had experienced two significant break-ups, both of whom I spent close to four years with. On both occasions, the relationships failed. Still, I had learnt many life lessons along the way, preparing me for this moment in my life with Sara.

It was now clear to me God had a plan. My previous relationships had broken down due to God's bigger plan for me.

What a beautiful day it was, surrounded by our loved ones, Sara and I made our intentions clear by performing the Fatiha – our journey of life was official. For the next three months, Sara and I were tied at the hip; her father had full confidence in me as I walked through the front door gaining his ultimate trust. The three months we shared before heading off to the US to face my next challenge were lovely. Sara was everything I had been searching for; she made me feel complete.

Now to get my career back on track. Set to face Garza, I had a tremendous camp. Things seemed so different this time around; having Sara in my life bought the best out of me. Back at the Foxwoods Resort, I remember asking my trainer Billy Hussein if I could share a few private words with him, 'Please, Billy … no matter what happens in this bout, if things turn for the worst do not stop this bout.' The memory of China had haunted me and I never wanted to experience another feeling like it again.

Everything in the bout went according to plan. I boxed smartly, avoiding all of Garza's power shots, securing a clear-cut unanimous decision and putting myself back in the winners' column. I was back. Life could not get any better. I was a winner, not only in the squared circle, but also in my love life. I couldn't wait to get back to Australia so I could pick up where I left off with Sara. I had been away from her for close to three weeks and speaking via telephone and Facebook wasn't cutting it.

Back home and the excitement started. The month of August would be one full of celebration. First, my birthday on 17 August, where I would turn twenty-nine years young – then 31 August where Sara and I would get engaged. What a beautiful night it was. Sara looked perfect in her stunning red gown, her beautiful ocean blue eyes shining; I was officially in love. We shared with those we loved most. The Bankstown Emporium hosted the beautiful night of our engagement, and later down the line, would host my return to boxing following the passing of Sara due to leukaemia.

The next thirteen months were indeed memorable; our relationship had its ups and downs, but one thing was for sure, we always managed to find a way to forgive each other at the end of every night.

After many beautiful months, Sara and I would once again be apart. This time, Sara and her family were off on the trip of a lifetime. Sara dreamt of celebrating New Year's Eve in New York. Her father wanted to make this a reality for Sara before we got married and started our journey together, but before all of this, Sara and I would share one of the most beautiful moments in life. I was set to make my return after a two-year absence from boxing in Australia. On 3 July 2014, I would make my return to home soil three months after beating Garza. This time I would be facing a durable Indonesian who had thirteen victories from twenty-four outings. Ruben Manakane would be the man standing in the opposite corner.

Scheduled for ten rounds, this fight would end with a devastating KO in the eighth, but this win didn't come easy. Let me take you on the journey of this bout. On the morning of the weigh-in, it seemed I wasn't going to make it to Melbourne where this fight would take place live on Fox Sports. I was sick and bedridden, struggling to weigh-in at the agreed 59kg. Billy Hussein decided to have the bout moved to the lightweight division, making things a little easier. After weighing in at the compromised weight of 61kg, it was time to replenish. Still, I couldn't hold anything down. I was too sick, and promoter Tarik Solak was adamant I pull out. However, I was determined to fight, as Sara and her family had made the trip to Melbourne to watch me. Tarik took me to see a doctor who indicated I had caught a bug and would need to get on a drip, as well as taking medication, with no promises I would be able to compete. But I was determined.

This bug had been in my system for a few days, but I hadn't known.

The day I was set to fly to Melbourne, I woke up at 2am feeling sick. I tried my best to get to the outdoor bathroom, as I didn't want my mother or father waking up and hearing me vomit, as I knew they wouldn't let me board the flight. After being sick, I woke up on the bathroom floor in shock. I had fainted due to being so dehydrated trying to cut to the super featherweight limit of 59kg.

I tried to make my way back to my room without waking anyone, only to faint once again, this time banging my head on my bedroom wall. My mother woke in fright finding me sprawled on the floor. She forced me to drink water and was adamant I had something to eat. I tried to explain to her I needed to weigh in at 59kg, but she wouldn't listen. She threatened to wake my father if I did not eat. If that were to happen, I had no hope of getting on the flight. I messaged Billy Hussein explaining the situation, and it was at that point he worked on having the bout moved to the lightweight division.

After a night of hell, I recovered and replenished on my way to scoring a sensational victory, especially considering the circumstances that had transpired.

The next day I shared a day I would never forget with Sara and my cousins, who had made the trip to Melbourne to support me. We created beautiful memories we always remembered if Sara and I were ever upset with each other.

Arriving back in Sydney, I was back on the grind. My next bout was 6 December, so I didn't have much time. This time, I would be facing heavy-handed Isaias Santos Sampaio for the vacant PABA super featherweight crown. A win would land me inside the top ten, guaranteeing me another opportunity at a world championship.

Sampaio had an impressive sixteen KOs from sixteen wins, and although he had a few losses, I would need to be 100% focused as a loss here could be detrimental.

As the bell rings, it's on! I was wary of Sampaio and boxed a very calculated round one, taking no risks. I was heading back to the corner for some instructions from Billy, who was very pleased with my patience in round one. I had ten rounds to break Sampaio down, so I was in no rush. During the prep for the bout, Billy and I continuously worked on the check left hook, and what do you know, at forty-eight seconds into round two that same shot presented itself – BOOM, down goes Sampaio like a tonne of bricks, the referee waved the fight off right away. Billy Hussein and the fight doctor rushed into the ring. Sampaio was back on his feet, and in a bizarre twist, the ref let the fight go on. Less than a minute later, I dropped Sampaio again to become the PABA Champion moving my record to thirty-eight wins from forty-two starts with twenty-two KOs.

The joy of victory is something not too many people can attest to. Competing in a combat sport is not like a team sport where you can lose one week and redeem yourself the next. Each fight takes weeks, sometimes months, of preparation, so this feeling of joy is something you can only feel two to three times a year, if you're lucky.

I was well and truly back in the mix of big-time boxing; I had worked my way back into the world rankings scoring three consecutive wins, placing me in the top ten with the IBF, WBA and WBC world rankings.

With Sara and her family set to head to the US, in what would be Sara's last official holiday, I took advantage of spending as much time with her as I could. I hated being away from her, but I was happy she was ticking off one of her life goals of spending New Year's Eve in NY at Times Square.

In a last-minute decision, I decided I would also take a trip to the US, heading in a completely different direction to Sara. Meeting with friend Matt Hilliard, we set off to Vegas to watch Amir Khan battle

Devon Alexander for the WBC silver title.

On 13 December, Sara was off on her trip of a lifetime. Going from state to state, eventually landing in New York for New Year's Eve, she was living out her dreams. By random chance, on 12 December, as I got off my flight from Sydney to LA, I was in transit heading to Vegas when I randomly ran into Sara and my cousin who was on the trip with Sara's family. It was such a beautiful surprise. I remember asking Sara if I could take pictures of her amazing eyes. I had become obsessed with her eyes, especially after watching a movie on my flight to LA called *I Origins*. The movie was based on a biologist in love with a woman who had the most beautiful eyes, but tragically died. He set off to India to find a girl who had the exact same eyes as the women who had passed away. This movie, and ocean blue eyes, were to have an impact on my life in more ways than one.

After the surprising catch up, I said my goodbyes and made my way to the terminal to catch the last leg of my flight. I was looking forward to catching up with Matt and watching Amir Khan in action.

I arrived into Vegas in time to catch the public weigh-in, where some of America's best talent was being showcased. I took the opportunity to reconnect with the face of Golden Boy Promotions, Oscar De La Hoya and Eric Gomez to discuss the possibility of resigning with the promotional powerhouse. Although nothing eventuated at the time, down the line, a great opportunity would present itself through the help of Eric Gomez.

What a fight night it was; an early glimpse of the Charlo Brothers, as well as the super-talented Errol Spence Jr – three fighters who would go to dominate the world of boxing in the years to follow. A childhood friend, Abner Mares, scored a dominant victory, then the main event where Amir Khan defeated Devon to win the WBC silver title. The love I received from boxing fans was inspiring. Rubbing shoulders with some of the world's best fighters was truly re-energising.

As the weeks passed, opportunities began presenting themselves. Three solid wins following my loss to Gradovich had placed me in position to challenge for world title honours once again. Sitting nicely at number five with the IBF and number ten with the WBC, I received offers to face both Jose Pedraza for the vacant IBF 130lb crown, as well as an offer to meet long-reigning WBC king, Takashi Miura. After back-and-forth negotiations with both camps, I decided to face Miura for the WBC crown. I felt it was an opportunity to win a championship that was robbed from Australia's own Jeff Fenech back in 1991, when he faced Azumah Nelson. It was an opportunity to right the wrongs and bring the crown back to Australia.

The opportunity to dethrone a reigning champion and the chance to go down in the history books as a two-weight three-division world champion was all the motivation I needed to dive headfirst into a gruelling training camp.

The date was set for 1 May 2015; a night that would go down in history for other reasons than my fight. A fight the world had been waiting for was finally set, Manny Pacquiao vs. Floyd Mayweather. On 2 March, I officially signed on to face Miura. This gave me precisely eight weeks to prepare to win the championship robbed from the hand of Australia's greatest fighter Jeff Fenech. The camp was underway, the team was assembled with Billy Hussein steering the ship, Hussein Hussein as the second assistant, Neil Dunkley as the strength coach and Brian Willmott, as always, the cutman. Billy began to source sparring partners who could mirror the southpaw style we were set to face against Miura.

Muira was a solid southpaw who possessed concussive power, scoring twenty-two KOs from twenty-eight wins; his bout against me would serve as his fifth defence.

I had no problem with Miura being a southpaw. I had faced over fifteen southpaws during my career as well as having the best southpaw sparring in the country, Paul Fleming, and long-time friend, Australian-based American Fred Tukes.

On 25 March, Billy decided to change things up to get a different look, inviting a different sparring partner who was a little taller than me. We were set to do six rounds, and moments into round two, Billy mentioned the name Sergio Martinez. In that exact moment, I switched to southpaw and threw an overhand left which landed flush and had me rolling on the canvas in agony. 'I've broken my hand!' I screamed. Billy quickly got in the ring and unlaced my glove. My hand looked like a bee had stung it. Neil promptly rushed me to the hospital. How could this be happening? Just when I thought my luck had turned.

After seeing the doctor, an X-ray was taken and we sat around waiting for the result. I knew deep down it was broken as the pain was excruciating. The only thing the X-ray would do was let us know how severe the break was. The doctor returned with the news I expected, 'You have broken a metacarpal in your left hand.'

I was heartbroken, although deep down I knew it was broken, I was hoping the doctor would bring back good news. I rang Billy, who urged me to stay positive and we would deal with it. I rang Sara, who played it down. 'Don't worry, everything happens for a reason,' she said. If I'm honest, her positivity didn't do much to stop the tears from flowing. My mother consoled me as she always did, but it didn't help.

What was hurting me the most was if I pulled out due to injury, I would not only lose the opportunity to capture the WBC crown, but the IBF had already removed me from the ratings, as I'd opted to face Miura rather than Pedraza for the IBF Strap.

The following morning, I received a call from both Billy and Neil who had come up with a plan. 'We are going through with the fight,' Billy said. His plan was for me to get a cortisone shot – 'It will mask the pain and help you get through camp.'

So, cortisone shot it was. After getting the hand sorted, I was back in the swing of training and sparring. I was feeling sharp and motivated. Having Neil around was a real plus as he had a very positive mindset, which rubbed off on me. He was also a complete genius when it came to my nutrition and helping me drop the weight.

Excitement was in the air. Fighting for the WBC Championship and being recognised as one of the best in the world, I was buzzing. With plenty of media attention surrounding my bout, Emaid managed to secure the fight on free-to-air TV on Channel 9 in Australia.

My bout against Miura would go live directly after the rugby league, meaning there would be a huge audience watching my fight, giving me the recognition I felt I deserved. This spurred me on to work even harder, to make history bringing the championship back to Australia.

The fight was a few weeks away; I felt most at ease when I was spending time with my fiancée Sara and my family. With so much to look forward to in life, it was an extremely exciting opportunity to make Australian boxing history, as well as marrying the love of my life on 5 December. Life was beautiful.

On Tuesday 21 April, just ten days out from my bout with Miura, the unthinkable would occur. Something didn't sit right that afternoon; I had forgotten my boxing boots – something that had never happened in my entire career. And I wasn't feeling well. It was as though God was giving me a sign it wasn't a good day to spar. Sparring with future IBF super bantamweight world champion TJ Doheny, a man I had worked with in the past, would end in disaster when he stuck me with a right rip from the southpaw stance, breaking my left rib cage.

I immediately stopped, telling TJ, 'You've broken my rib.' I was in such good condition that even after breaking my rib, I managed to stay on my feet despite the excruciating pain.

I couldn't believe my luck. First the hand, now my rib. What was next? I was devastated. Surely now the fight would be called off. If I pulled out I'd be back to square one, but only a madman would enter the ring against a wrecking machine like Miura with a broken rib. I had a lot of thinking to do, with not much time to decide. Waking up the following morning, I wasn't feeling good. Neil popped by, picking me up before heading back to the hospital to get a scan taken to see how severe the damage was. It wasn't right. I asked the doctor if getting a cortisone shot would help, but his response was a blunt: 'No, unfortunately, the only thing you can do is allow it to heal. I suggest you pull the pin on this fight.'

How could I? Other than my direct team, no-one understood the position I was. Pulling out would mean I would lose both opportunities with the WBC and the IBF. The doctor made one suggestion, 'When it pops out just lift your arm and it will pop back in.' He advised me to ice it regularly and be sure not to cop any more knocks on it before the bout.

Truth is, I was in such a positive mind state, I didn't think about the injuries much. They were always in the back of my mind, but that's where I left them. Set to depart, I met with Sara urging her not to worry and I would see her soon as the new WBC Champion of the World. She was very supportive but wanted me to know, boxing title or not, she loved me unconditionally.

I arrived in Japan greeted by many members of the media; there was excitement in the air. I had an excellent support team in Japan, headed by my siblings and a few of my relatives, as well as good friends Paula, Michael and Matt who made the long trip from San Francisco; I was feeling the love.

With the bout just two days away, Miura and I would face off for the first time at the official press conference. I was in great spirits and 'ready to rumble'. The following day, the weigh-in took place. Billy and Neil had done an excellent job in the lead-up, making sure my weight was on point. Both Miura and I weighed in on the super featherweight limit of 58.97kg. I was ripped and ready. The stare-down took place; I sized him up, shook his hand and was on my way. My confidence was sky-high. I couldn't wait to hear those words every fighter lives to hear: '… AND THE NEW …'

On fight day, I woke up in a very positive state of mind, surrounded by family and friends. I spent the majority of the day reflecting on my camp and all I had overcome to arrive at this point. A broken hand and broken rib. One thing was for sure, the journey wasn't an easy one. With Brian Willmott in my corner, I was confident my hand wouldn't be an issue, as I had complete confidence in Brian's work. He had wrapped my hands in every fight to this point.

After a relaxed day, we headed to the Ota-City General Gymnasium venue, where the bout would take place. We arrived in time for Maghrib prayers; I asked the Almighty to allow both Miura and I to leave the ring safely and to grant me the victory, if it would be good for me. With the fight crossing live to Australia via Channel 9, Mark Warren accompanied the team to cover all media. Moments before heading out to face Miura, we crossed 'live' and super excited, I told the Australian public I would do all I could to dethrone Miura and bring the championship home.

I was completely relaxed, listening to LL Cool J's 'Mama Said Knock You Out' as I made my ring walk. I stepped through the ropes and circled the ring. With Miura and I now standing on opposite sides, it was time for the national anthems. With the instructions read, we touched gloves and it was on.

Ding-ding, the fight was underway. Miura attacked as I immediately started circling to my left to avoid his mighty left hand. During the first minute, Miura stalked but I kept him at bay with my superior hand and foot speed. Landing a few good shots, as well as my trademark Prince Naseem lunging uppercut, I was on my way to winning round one. At 132 seconds into round one, Miura pinned me on the ropes and fired a barrage of shots to my ribs.

Did he know about my injury? Nevertheless, I was back on my bike sticking Miura with the jab. He had a menacing look on his face as he landed a few more good shots to my body at 1:03 of the round. At this point on the footage, you can see me rubbing my left ribcage. During the last minute of round one, I began to land some clean punches sticking to the plan of protecting my ribcage and chin, as Miura's power was definately an equaliser. Round one ends and Billy H, as well as my brothers, Emaid and Mohammed, were delighted as I had followed the instructions to a tee.

With round two underway, I was immediately back on the jab, as well as landing a flush right uppercut. I tied Miura up before he had a chance to counter. His right eye was beginning to show signs of swelling, but it didn't stop him from stalking relentlessly. At 1:22 of round two, after trading blows with each other, I lifted my left arm to pop my rib cage back into place, as my surgeon back home had advised me. It was safe to say I had banked the first two rounds on the three judge's cards.

Going back to the corner, I told Billy H, 'This is easy work.'

With an angry voice, Billy said, 'Do not underestimate him, he is no joke. Stay focused and DO NOT GET COCKY.'

'Okay, Billy,' I responded. 'I'm focused.'

Round three commenced with the same pattern: Miura stalking and me sticking and moving. If I could stick to the plan, I could take the WBC title back to Australia. At 2:20 of round three, Miura jabs and I counter jab, but my dam rib cage won't give me a break. Miura fired his left hand with some bad intentions. Woosh, it flew over my head as I ducked. At 1:57 Miura pins me on the ropes and fires bombs at my rib cage again. I back-pedalled away, but he kept coming. At 1:48 of round three, Miura landed a concussive left hand. It was the shot he'd been looking for in the first two rounds. As I was falling to the canvas, Miura landed a further two blows, leaving me in a daze.

I looked up at the bright lights thinking, *I have to get up.* I somehow got to my feet as the ref counts. 'Come to me,' he calls. I don't respond. 'Come to me,' he repeats. I try to walk straight but take a slight shuffle to my left, forcing the referee to stop the bout.

Billy H and my brothers run to my aid. 'I'm okay.' The only thing hurting me was the fact I'd blown this great opportunity. I looked up at the screen seeing the final three blows which put an end to the bout.

How did I manage to get back up? It was as though the Almighty God had given me the strength to end the bout on my feet, to avoid the embarrassment of being knocked out.

I credited this to my team who had helped me get into excellent condition.

I was devastated. We left the ring only to be bombarded by members of the media. I could also see Emaid walking towards me with his phone, trying to pass it to me. 'Sara is on the line,' he said. She was in tears. I assured her I was okay and not to worry. I answered a few questions from the media and spoke to my parents before making my way to get showered up.

I finally got a chance to sit and reflect on what happened. On the ride back to the hotel, I thanked everyone for their efforts and apologised for letting this ample opportunity slip away. As I stepped off the bus, Billy H and I shared a chat. Billy wanted me to prepare myself for some negative comments that would come my way after the devastating loss. Truth is, I was not concerned about what people thought. I was proud to have represented my family and country at the highest level.

Upon landing back in Australia, I headed to the Channel 9 headquarters; we discussed my opinion on what transpired in my bout with Miura, as well as the match-up between Floyd Mayweather and Manny Pacquiao.

Back in the car, I made my way home to see my family and my beautiful fiancée, Sara.

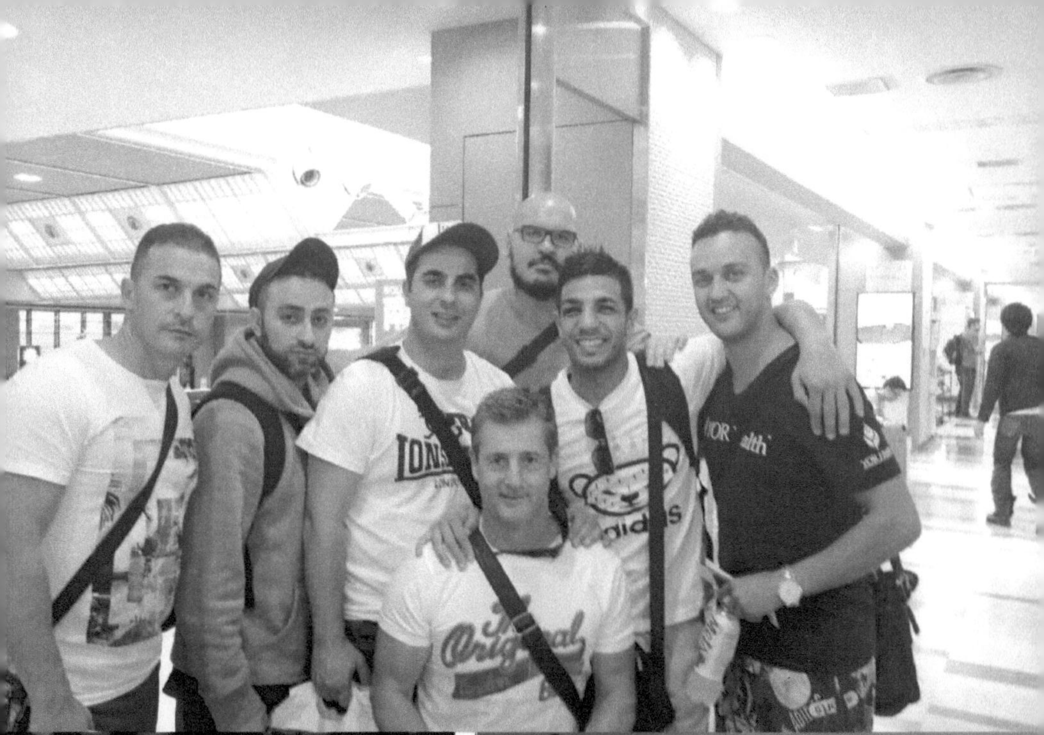

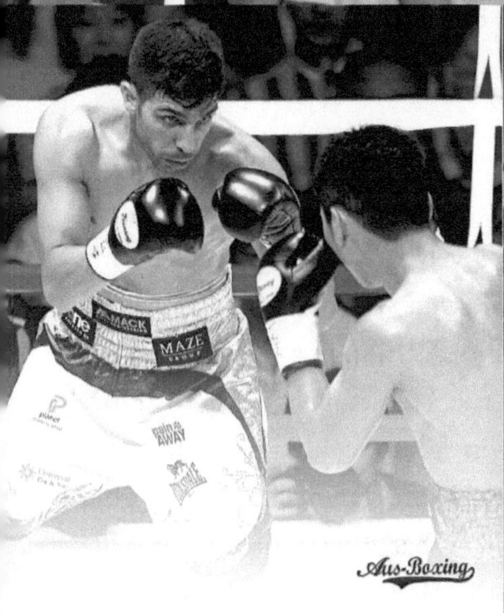
Aus-Boxing

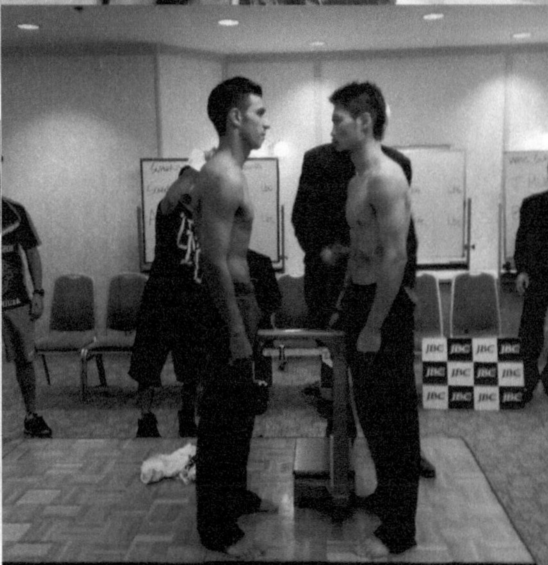

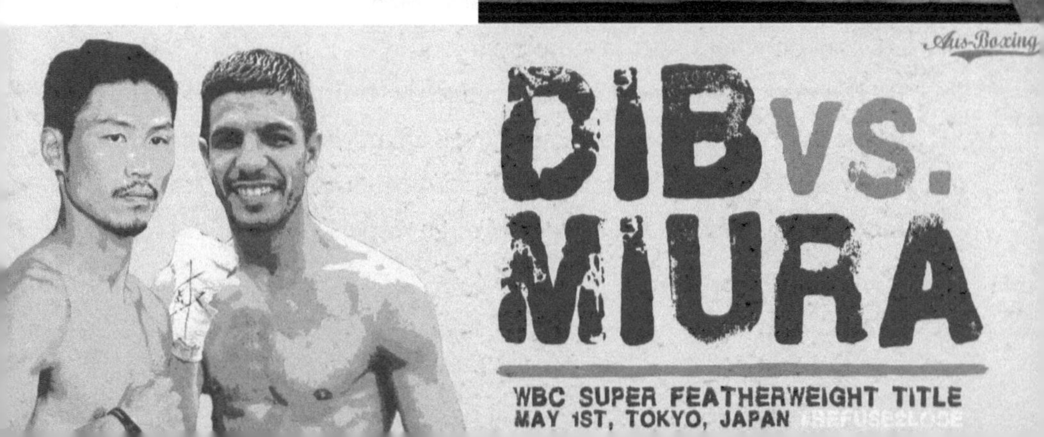
Aus-Boxing
DIB VS.
MIURA
WBC SUPER FEATHERWEIGHT TITLE
MAY 1ST, TOKYO, JAPAN

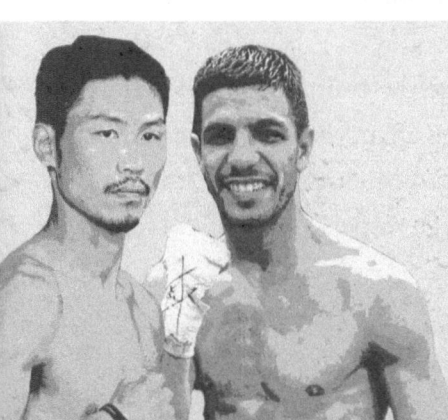

CHAPTER SEVENTEEN
SARA

I remember the day vividly; it was so lovely to be back home with my family. We all sat in the lounge room and watched on as Floyd put on a master class, winning a wide points decision in a fight billed 'The Fight of the Millennium'. Thinking back, I remember feeling so empty as I watched Floyd cruise to an easy win, as all I could think about was how I had missed my opportunity to win the famous green and gold WBC crown. What would I do next? What direction could my life now take? One thing was for sure, we can plan, but as we plan God also has a say on what's next in store for us.

The next few months would change the course of my life forever. Let me take you on the journey of how it all unfolded. Towards the end of May 2015, friends of mine, Paula and Michael, felt life in front of the camera as a sports commentator might serve as a good idea for me.

They introduced me to Billy Milionis, a mad boxing fan and owner of a successful acting school called The Actor's Pulse.

After several years of boxing wars, where I'd received my fair share of cuts and bruises, I decided to get some voluntary surgery to clean up the scar tissue around my eyes and nose. A few weeks before going into surgery, I remember being in the gym on a treadmill beside my brother Emaid. I discussed a plan with him about flying to the US to meet with American-based promoter Lou DiBella about another possible run at a championship. Emaid wasn't keen on the plan and pleaded with me to wrap up my career and concentrate on life with Sara, moving in a new direction. I could tell he was serious, as he also mentioned he would give me a large sum of money to start a venture so I wouldn't need to box again.

I could understand his concern. I knew he was also speaking on behalf of my father and mother, as well as Sara, but boxing made me happy. It made me feel alive.

On 27 May, my surgery was done. It was a step in the right direction as it would help if I decided to take part in any future fights. The years of fighting had left me with damaged scar tissue around my eyes that would open and bleed at the slightest punch. Now with the surgery, I knew I'd be able to fight again without having that problem.

After getting back from Tokyo, Sara and I were on quite a rollercoaster in regard to our relationship. Just like every couple, we had our fair share of ups and downs. It seemed we would take ten steps forward than fifteen back and I felt this was due to the pressure of our upcoming wedding on 6 December.

Sara was regularly getting sick and always complaining saying how tired and sleepy she was. This made me feel she didn't want me around. She was visiting the doctors regularly and their only advice was to, 'Get some rest. You're okay.' During this time, Sara developed a lump on her neck that would appear and disappear from time to time. On 16 July Sara's mother booked an appointment with a specialist to get to the bottom of this reoccurring lump. Upon our arrival to the specialist, Sara seemed to be in good spirits. The doctor mentioned it was most likely her lymph nodes were swollen. A biopsy was taken, and we were told they would contact us in a few days to give us the results.

Sara headed home to get some rest, and I headed home to carry on with my day. Shortly after arriving home, I received a call from Sara telling me the specialist had called her back. I pleaded with Sara to wait for me so I could accompany her. Sara being Sara, not wanting to burden me, was adamant she and her mother would go and call me later to keep me in the loop. I felt uneasy but agreed. I felt very uncomfortable about it, but Sara didn't seem to be concerned.

Less than an hour later, I was in the lounge room of my family home patiently waiting, when I received the call from Sara I was waiting for. 'Babe ... what are you doing?' she asked.

'Just lounging ... waiting to hear from you,' I responded. At this point, Sara dropped the bomb that would change the course of both our lives.

The next words spoken, 'I have cancer,' left me gobsmacked.

'What? Are you joking?' I responded. Sara broke down hysterically. Her mother, Gada, took the phone and asked me to make my way to their home. My mother, standing directly in front of me listening in on the phone call, broke down in tears. As a family, we were no strangers to cancer, as my uncle Haisam had succumbed to cancer two decades earlier, back in 1993.

I immediately got into my car and drove to Cronulla. As I drove to Sara's home, a million thoughts went through my head. There was one image I couldn't seem to shake off. It was the moment my mother heard me say 'cancer'; her instant reaction was to cover her face with both hands and say, 'OH MY GOD, SHE'S GOING TO DIE.'

Sara had a timid placid personality, she wasn't much of a fighter, hence the reason I think my mother said what she did. I know God does things for a reason, but I couldn't help but think, *Why Sara? She's so young with so much life to live.* These were the thoughts ringing in my mind. In that moment, I truly wished it was me. The reason I felt that way is because I'm a fighter. I'd been fighting since the day my mother gave birth to me; I was born to be a fighter. My mother was a fighter herself. And my father was a man who sacrificed his whole life, to give his growing family a chance to be 'somebodies' in this world.

CHAPTER EIGHTEEN
MY MOTHER

My mother, a Palestinian girl, born on 14 July 1957, was raised in Beirut, Lebanon. She has faced many trials throughout her life. When she was nineteen years old, her beloved father, Hassan Mubarak, passed away in tragic circumstances when a fishing trip went wrong; TNT on the boat caught alight, blowing my grandfather into pieces. Less than four years later, tragedy would strike again. This time, my mother's youngest brother, Nasser, was murdered in a coffee shop, in cold blood, at just seventeen years old. Not even a month would pass before the man who murdered my uncle would himself be killed. Although this would not rid my mother of her pain, it was good for her to know that the man who took her brother's life no longer existed in the world.

Lebanon had been at war during the mid-1970s so my mother was no stranger to bombings and seeing people die. During these difficult years of her life, my mother would see things that would mortify any young teen. When I was a young boy, she would often tell me stories of how she would hide her siblings during bombings and fend solders off from entering her family home in a bid to protect her younger brothers and sisters. My mother was, and is, a real fighter. As kids in our society, we have been brainwashed through various TV shows to look at fictional superheroes such as Batman, Superman, Superwoman and so on to be our heroes. I didn't have to look far. In my eyes, my superheroes were my mother and father, for different reasons.

My father made sacrifices to bring his whole family from Lebanon to Australia. My mother made sacrifices in leaving her mother, siblings and relatives behind to start a new life in Australia. She had also faced real hardship and heartbreak in her life.

Growing up, I felt my mother was a real-life Jackie Chan. I was seven or eight years old when an unforgettable event took place, while my mother took my brother Nasser and me for a walk. During our walk, a man attacked us from behind screaming racial slurs at my mother telling her to 'go back to your own country' while trying to rip her headscarf from her head. With the safety of her children at risk, the protector in my mother shined through as she kicked and punched the racist man.

I saw my mother differently after this incident: my mother, my protector, my real-life superhero. I am a fighter through and through, and I feel a lot of this has been instilled in me through my mother's blood. She is a strong Palestinian and I am her son; the fighters' blood is a part of my DNA.

The drive to Sara's felt like a lifetime; it seemed like I got stuck at every red light on the way. What would I say to the girl I had fallen in love with when I saw her? How was I supposed to handle this situation? I finally arrived. I parked the car and nervously made my way to her front door. I rang the doorbell. Gada opened the door and greeted me. She looked as though she'd been crying. I walked into the lounge room. Sara was seated in front of the heater, curled up like a ball. It broke my heart; she looked so deflated. I asked her to stand up and I hugged her and told her not to worry; we would beat this.

It was my responsibility to keep Sara's spirits high. I was her husband to be and needed to be a rock for her. 'People survive cancer every day. You'll be fine. We will fight this together – one round at a time.' As the night set in the mood eased. I spent most of the afternoon and evening with Sara and her family. Tomorrow was a new day and Eid, a day of celebration to mark the end of Ramadam for all Muslims around the world. I was a little worried as I didn't want Sara to feel like she needed to be explaining herself to every relative who tried to bring it up. I wasn't going to allow anyone to upset her.

I left Sara's home at around 10:30pm and she seemed to be in higher spirits as we spent the night sharing jokes, easing the atmosphere. Upon arriving at home, I received a text message from Sara.

I just wanted to say thank you for all your love today and just being there.

My response:

Today was a hard day for you, but I was so proud of how you handled yourself. You being sick changes nothing, what doesn't break us makes us stronger. Sara, I know the next four to six months will be a battle, but I will be there every step of the way. We are in a twelve-round battle you and I will fight each round at a time. We won't lose any rounds because we are winners. Remember this, what you think will magnify so only think positive thoughts. We have been through the wringer, but we are still fighting. Love you very much let the battle begin we are ready.

Looking back now, the response I got back from Sara was somewhat of a message reminding me that no matter what happens, life must go on. It was as if she already felt she wasn't going to make it.

I love you too but promise me you will take every opportunity that comes your way ... as you said me being sick changes nothing. I want you to pursue your dreams and regret nothing. Don't let what's going on with me change that. I know I have your support every step of the way, even oceans apart. Be my motivation to keep on fighting no matter what tries to knock you down along the way.

I tried my best to lift Sara's spirits with my final response.

Don't worry about all that. Just give me a favour and be strong, and no matter how hard this fight gets, fight as hard as you can. Whatever happens, I'm in this with you till we knock it on its ass – Sleep well. Goodnight.

The following morning 17 July 2015, the day of Eid, I woke up to join my father, brother and a few of my relatives at Lakemba mosque for Eid prayers. I spoke to my cousins, Reyad and Shereef about Sara's condition, asking them to make dua, a special prayer asking assistance from God that Sara would overcome this horrible disease.

Upon finishing the prayers, my cousins and I headed back to my Aunty Hoda and Uncle Hussam's home to participate in Eid celebrations, as we had done for as long as I can remember. I was eager to see Sara as I got closer to my aunty's home. I saw Sara's car. There she was, looking so angelic, so beautiful and natural. *How could she possibly have cancer?* These were the thoughts going through my mind. Putting on a brave face, I could see the pain in her eyes, and she carried herself with so much class and elegance, not wanting her sickness to affect anyone's day.

I wanted to do all I could to put a smile on Sara's face. My family members and relatives went above and beyond to make sure Sara had a wonderful day. The weeks that followed after finding out about Sara's condition were kind of quiet. I was attending acting school as well as keeping in contact with boxing promoters worldwide. I had always shared a reasonably close relationship with American-based promoter Lou Diabella throughout my career. Although he thought it was best I retire after my most recent loss to Muira, I convinced him to give me another opportunity. I knew I still could mix it with the world's elite super featherweights. After weeks of back-and-forth conversations with Lou, he presented me with a plan. He would give me another opportunity, but it would come with one condition, he wanted me to be assessed by a trainer of his choice. This trainer would be the world-renowned Ronnie Shields.

Ronnie was an accomplished amateur boxer who had competed and won Golden Glove championships in 1976 and 1978. Later turning professional in 1980, he challenged for world championship honours in 1984 and 1986. Unfortunately, both attempts were unsuccessful. Although Ronnie was a good fighter, it was as a trainer he would blossom, working with some big names and producing many world champions. Lou said if I flew to Houston and allowed Ronnie to assess me through a short training camp, he would consider signing me up, only if Ronnie found me fit to compete at the highest level.

I agreed to this but would need to work out a time. Sara had an essential appointment with Professor Mark Hertzberg on 30 July. This was to discuss the severity of her cancer and how far it had travelled, as well as the approach he would take to tackle Sara's condition. On the day, I joined Sara and her parents, Ibby and Gada, for the appointment with Professor Hertzberg. I remember vividly the words Mark Hertzberg would say.

'Sara, you have been diagnosed with T-cell lymphoma leukaemia. You are young and healthy, so you will overcome this. It will be a marathon, but you will be fine.'

He discussed that Sara would be an inpatient, staying in hospital full-time during her treatment. He also addressed the potential side effects from the treatment, with a possibility of blood clots, heart failure or pancreas failure. Though as Sara was young and healthy, he was sure none of the above would occur. It was all so real now. Everything had been confirmed. We knew what the procedure would be. Sara's stay would start on 11 August 2015. I had decided to fly to Houston on 3 August and be back in time to be there with Sara as she started her hospital journey.

Upon leaving the hospital, the mood was very quiet. I looked at Sara, knowing how much I loved her and how I wanted to spend the rest of my life with her. We all got back into the car. Sara and I sat in the back seat where I held her hand, telling her I wanted to marry her. She smiled and said: 'God willing … once I'm better and my hair has grown back.'

'No,' I responded, 'now. Uncle Ibby, we need to get married.'

'Just be patient,' was his reply. 'We will talk about it.'

When we arrived back at my home, Ibby asked me to see him the following day after Friday prayers. In that moment, not being married to Sara before she entered the hospital was not an option for me. I loved her and wanted her to know I would be right by her side, through thick and thin.

Before meeting with Ibby, I needed to discuss my plan with my father and mother. I spoke of my intentions and reasons. My parents supported my decision and applauded me for being an honourable man. I remember the date as though it was yesterday: 31 July 2015. I was not at all nervous, I knew what I wanted. After praying at Lakemba Mosque, I drove towards Cronulla stopping at my future father-in-law's travel agency in Caringbah. As soon as I arrived, Ibby closed the doors and we sat down to have a real heart to heart. Ibby was very open. He spoke to me about the seriousness of this cancer and the fact that Sara may never be able to have children due to the chemo. I responded by telling Ibby I didn't care. I loved Sara, and if God had written for us to have children, nothing would stop it. And if not, well, it didn't matter as I loved Sara and certainly wouldn't bail on her because she couldn't have children. After a few hours of back-and-forth discussions, Uncle Ibby agreed Sara and I would be married on the following Sunday, giving us just two days to prepare a wedding ceremony. The biggest reason behind my decision was I wanted to be by Sara's side without being a third wheel during her stay in hospital, as without being married, I was required to be chaperoned every time I was with her. I was so excited and happy. Ibby gave me a big hug and told me he would allow me to break the news to Sara, her mother and siblings. Off to Sara's house to propose. I was so excited.

I arrived at Sara's home and knocked on the door. I was greeted by Gada who invited me in as Sara made her way downstairs and sat down. I got down on one knee and asked her if she would marry me. She laughed and said, 'Yes … when I get better.'

'No,' I said, 'this Sunday.' I told Sara about how I'd spoken with her father, and he agreed to allow us to get married during these challenging circumstances.

Sara began to cry. 'Yes, I will marry you,' she said, as she told me, 'I love you,' with tears flowing from her eyes. Her mother was also in tears, as her firstborn would fulfil her dream of getting married. I couldn't hang around for too long as I needed to get home and share the good news with my family and organise a guest list, contacting all my loved ones to see if they would be able to join us on this day special. My parents were over the moon.

I broke the news to my siblings and closest cousins. It was all happening so fast; in two days I would be a married man. Everything flowed so perfectly, everyone we called confirmed they would be there on Sunday. I would be a married man to a beautiful girl, and I couldn't wait. Sunday arrived and we had managed to put together a ceremonial wedding. I was so proud of the effort my family had put in to make the day possible. It all seemed to go by so fast, and before I knew it, the guests were flowing in. Sara looked so elegant. She was a little nervous but thrilled the moment had arrived. The Sheike arrived and the ceremony started. It was all happening so fast, our lives as one had just begun. Surrounded by our loved ones, it was perfect. After the celebrations, Sara and I headed out to town as a married couple. My wife; wow, it felt so surreal. I would spend the rest of my life with this beautiful soul.

One of my biggest regrets was I didn't get to spend the night with Sara, as I had previously organised my flight to Houston, Texas, to join Ronnie Shields for the 'assessment' week that same night. I wish I could turn back time, so we could have spent the week together before Sara went into hospital. After a night out, I dropped Sara off at home and told her I would see her before I left for Houston. 11:53pm I received a picture message from Sara; it was the flowers I had bought her, and she had written *luckiest girl* beneath the picture. *Most beautiful girl,* I responded.

Goodnight love of my life so happy you're finally my husband XX I love you.

The next morning Sara met me at the airport. We spent some time together before I was set to depart. Before take-off, I sent a message to Sara:

Love you very much thank you so much for everything and for understanding why I need to do this.

Don't thank me, babe, of course, I understand. You'll be back home before we know it. Just enjoy yourself and do what you gotta do.

She was so understanding and appreciated my love for boxing. She wanted me to continue to chase my dreams and never live with regret. I set upon this journey with my teammate, a close friend Billel Dib, yeah yeah, we both share the same name. Upon arriving at Houston, Billel and I were joined by my good friend Matt Hilliard. We checked into the hotel and headed to the plex gym. Ronnie trained a solid stable of fighters, including the Charlo Brothers, who still dominate the middleweight ranking today.

I aimed to do all I could to impress Ronnie; enough for him to notify Lou I still possessed the goods to compete at the highest level in the sport of boxing. There was not much downtime, as Ronnie had us booked into a very strenuous seven-day camp. Although I was in Houston trying to resurrect my career, my heart and mind was in Sydney, Australia, with my beloved wife, Sara. Part of why I was doing all this was to ensure I could still earn money from the sport to give us a good life. I arrived in Houston on Monday the 3rd and started training right away. The week would consist of sparring, running, weights and explosive hand-eye coordination drills. I can honestly say I gave it my all, leaving a good impression as I promised I would. After a solid week, it was time to head back to Australia to be by Sara's side. Her treatment started on 12 August.

As soon as I landed in Sydney on the 12th, I rushed out of the airport and headed directly home to be by Sara's side. I remember driving to the hospital. I was so nervous yet so excited to see my wife. Sara was to face the most challenging battle of her young life, and I wanted to do all I could to help her overcome this horrible cancer. I arrived at Prince of Wales hospital, the place that would become Sara's home for the next few months. I parked the car and headed to the cancer ward, room 10 W bed 11. I walked in as Sara was about to have her lumber spine injection. I made it only in the nick of time to hold Sara's hand and support her through this painful ordeal.

I remember holding Sara's hand. She was sweating profusely, yet she was so brave and handled it like the true champion she was. Once the injection was done, I gave both Sara and her mother a hug. I tried to change the mood, filling Sara in about my trip and all the exciting things that took place during my time in Houston. After spending the day at the hospital with Sara, I gave her a goodnight hug and kiss and headed home to get some much-needed rest. I was so jet-lagged.

The coming months would all be about Sara. Everything would be put on hold, and my sole focus was to be by my wife's side. I guess the most upsetting part of all this was that Sara and I couldn't spend our nights together, as I was only allowed to be at the hospital from 8am to 8pm. Every day was the same; wake up, drive to the hospital, play Uno, watch movies, lay down and keep Sara company. This was on repeat for the many weeks to come. Before Sara entered the hospital, I asked her to purchase a book to document her journey; I have her final thoughts. She would consistently write that the chemo would be the end of her. She always wrote '*so-and-so* days until doomsday' as if she knew her days in this life were numbered. Day five of Sara's hospital stay is a day I'll never forget. My cousin Sara Shami and I decided to take Sara out to the movies. The choice of film was a disaster. During the trailers of movies set to come out in the coming months, one was a trailer about a girl with leukaemia.

To make matters worse, it was based on a true story. Sara turned her face and burst into tears. She was devastated. I pleaded with her that we should leave, but she was adamant we stay. I held Sara close, holding her hand and cuddling her throughout the movie. Dropping Sara off at the end of the night was always hard. She wore sunglasses a lot, not to be cool, but to hide her tears. She would never say so, but I could see she was hurting. Driving home alone after being with Sara killed me. I wanted to be there to make sure she was okay. Over the coming weeks, Sara would slowly decline in health. Little did I know, the last time I would walk hand-in-hand with Sara in a public place, would be Bondi. It was one of Sara's favourite locations. I'm glad Sara and I, alongside my cousin Shereef and his wife Jamila, would be blessed to share her last hospital outing. On the night of 5 September, Sara suffered a horrific seizure that would land her in the ICU. The doctors told us Sara was doing well, so this all came as quite a shock and was a lot to deal with.

In the weeks leading up to the seizure, Sara was continually complaining of headaches and migraines. She discovered iced coffee helped, which indicated she had an issue with the chemo treatment. When Sara was having the seizure, I was at my older brother Emaid's house accompanied by my cousin Reyad, watching the NRL dragons, the team we all supported. When the game was done, I said my goodbyes to head for home. As soon as I got into my car, I received a call from Sara's mother, who stressed for me to get to the hospital immediately, as Sara was suffering a seizure. I froze. Was this the end? How could I have left the hospital so early? How could something like this happen? I had made a promise always to be there to protect Sara and look out for her.

After getting stuck at nearly every red light, I finally arrived at the hospital. I rushed to the ICU ward to see Sara, who at this point was not herself. She looked exhausted and lost. The seizure had caused Sara to lose her ability to speak and communicate as she had previously done. I was extremely upset to see what had happened to Sara, and making matters worse was the fact that nobody could give us any answers.

The coming days were quite a challenge. I would arrive at the hospital at 8am and leave when the ICU ward would close for visitors. Sara's decline had become very apparent, and in a moment of desperation for Sara to come back to her complete senses, I tried to look for ways to communicate with her. I asked Sara if she knew I loved her. She seemed very confused as though she didn't understand me. I looked for something to write a message on, my boarding pass from my most recent trip to the US was in my bag. I pulled it out and wrote I LOVE YOU on it. I showed it to Sara. At that moment, she opened her hand, spreading her fingers in a gesture for me to lock hands with her; she understood what I had written.

The following night, Sara's father became very frustrated by her inability to communicate. Before leaving the hospital, he looked Sara directly in her eyes and said, 'LA ILAHA ILLALLAH. Tomorrow when I come back, I want to see you speak.'

As he made his way out of the ICU ward, she responded, saying, 'MUHAMMADUR RUSULULLAH.' (Muhammad is his Messenger.)

I was shocked Sara had finally spoken; I ran outside to notify Ibby that Sara was speaking. He came back to the room with me. I asked Sara to repeat herself; she responded by saying, 'LA ILAHA ILLALLAH.'

Sara's father began to cry. I wasn't sure if these were tears of joy or sadness. These were the last words Sara would speak. The following day I arrived at the hospital a little late. It seemed like just another day, but I was wrong. As I approached the ICU ward, I saw my Aunty Hoda in the distance. She appeared to be crying. I immediately ran towards the ICU ward knocking on the door violently. A nurse answered and refused to let me in. I wouldn't take no for an answer, arguing my wife was inside, only to be tackled to the floor by my brother Muhammad who pleaded with me to relax, saying Sara was okay. Moments later, Sara was wheeled past me with tubes and monitors hooked to her bed.

Sara had fallen into a coma. Was this now the beginning of the end? A few weeks before all this transpired, I felt the need to ask Sara if there was anything I could do for her. She responded with the most beautiful message. She was such a lovely, selfless, loving human being. Reading back through her diary shows how she was concerned about everyone but herself. Her response to my message was:

To the man of my dreams. Things may have started off a little rocky, and we could never see eye to eye. Honestly, at the start, it was hard for me to see a whole future with you. Hard work, love and commitment has paid off, and now I can't imagine my life with anyone else except you. Every time I think of my future with you, I can't help but smile. You make me so incredibly happy. Your stupid jokes, your humour, your smile, your voice, your hugs and kisses, your manner, your love is what I look forward to every day.

I can't wait to wake up every morning next to my best friend and lover.

What do I dream to have? Baby, we could be anywhere in the world, we could live in a shack and sleep on a mattress on the floor, and I wouldn't care. As long as I'm with you, and our love is strong. You make me the happiest girl in the world. I dream that you make wholehearted choices that make you happy. Baby, all I want is your happiness and love; I admire your accomplishments and everything you have achieved and will achieve continuously inshallah. But I'm not interested in that guy and never have been. I have fallen in love with a guy named Billy Dib. A guy who I can watch movies with eating pizza in a baggy shirt and trackie pants and will still call me beautiful when I'm not even trying. You can't help me find anything because I've already found what was meant for me. It amazes me that the love of my life was right underneath my nose the whole time, and I was so blind to see you. I want you and only you; I want all of your kisses, I want all of you. I want us forever and always. Love from your wife X

The days in the ICU depressed me. We prayed and prayed for a miracle. I felt so hopeless as Sara lay in the bed fighting for her life. The doctors told me it would be up to Sara to wake from this coma; day in, day out for a few weeks, I would talk to her, begging her to wake up as I would be lost without her. Sara had documented a daily diary, but as she was no longer able to write, I took it as my responsibility to document her journey, so I could read it to her when she woke up and was back to her senses. ALL WE HAVE IS HOPE.

After Sara's life-threatening operation, where a blood clot needed to be removed from the centre of her brain, Dr Raj Reedy told me he had been successful and was confident Sara would recover. I was overjoyed and couldn't wait to tell her about what she had overcome. Days after the operation, things would take a turn for the worst. There was a moment when Sara was being nursed that caused her much distress. It seemed that everything turned from that moment. The following day, Dr Hertzberg and his team sat us down as a family to explain they had done all they could for Sara. They expressed their regret in telling us they felt Sara would not make it, and only a miracle from God would bring her back. They offered to set up temporary accommodation in the hospital for us to stay with Sara and share her last moments on this Earth. I tried my best to hold myself together. Sara's father was so confused: 'What do you mean? Is it money? Because I'll pay anything … this is my daughter.'

The doctor's response would change my perception of money for the remainder of my life. 'Mr Selim, it's not money. No amount of money could save Sara … only a miracle.'

For some reason, all I could think about was my situation with Curtis Jackson (50 Cent) and the money I had lost.. What good would that be to me now? Even if I had the money, I couldn't use it to save Sara. So, from then on, I promised myself to let it go and let the Almighty and karma deal with Curtis Jackson. After the doctors left, I shed some tears but still had hope. Ibby looked me in the eyes and said, 'She will not leave us. She would not do that to me.' After leaving the room, I ran into Dr Raj Reedy. He took me around the corner away from all eyes and ears and showed me some scans. The scans showed Sara was brain dead; only the machine was keeping her alive.

'I'm not giving up,' I told him.

He explained that even if she woke up by some miracle, she would be brain dead and a vegetable. I was devastated but held myself together until arriving home and breaking down once I saw my mother. She slept by my side that night, as I cried myself to sleep while holding a picture of Sara. The next morning, I headed to the hospital. I promised Sara I would not leave her side, and for the next three days, I stayed with her. I would only leave the hospital to freshen up. Plenty of relatives and friends waited at the hospital, but to respect her wishes, no one was allowed to see Sara except for myself, her parents and my parents. One exception was my cousin Sara Shami, who was Sara's best friend. Sara had requested no-one see her if things turned for the worst, she wanted to be remembered for who she was. Saturday 26 September, Sara fought right to the very end; the doctors gave us a heads-up that Sara would not see the following day, so Saturday, what a day, was filled with endless tears and support from my loved ones.

I fell asleep on the ICU floor, beside Sara's bed. About 9pm, a nurse woke me, telling me Sara would be gone soon. Sara's father was reciting from the Holy Quran; he was reciting Surat Yasin.

It was so beautiful yet so sad; Sara was still fighting hard at 11:25pm. My cousin Reyad called me, telling me to leave the room as her soul would not leave her body if I remained present. I explained I had promised her I would not leave her side and minutes later, Sara's monitors began to shut down. I cried so much. *How is this happening? She looked fine before the damn chemo.* At 11:31pm, my beloved wife Sara had departed this world. Gada's words sent chills down my spine; 'My daughter is an angel.' At the moment she died, she turned porcelain white. 'Kiss her,' Gada said. I was so afraid to touch Sara once she'd died. I left the room to notify my relatives and loved ones that Sara was no longer with us, and she had returned to her creator. So many cries ran through the hospital. After the funeral service picked up Sara's body, I headed home. It all felt like a horrible dream; I was a broken man.

Upon arriving at home, I felt the need to shower and scrub my body so hard. I wanted to wash the horrible feeling away. I laid in bed and had my brother compose a message to share with my fans, notifying them Sara had sadly passed away.

Sara's eventual death came from a blood clot to the brain caused by the chemo. Sara was, in fact, in remission at the time of her death.

Saturday 26 September – the most challenging night of my life, I don't remember sleeping for even one minute. Sunrise came, and in only a few hours, my family home was filled with loved ones who would accompany us to the morgue where we would wash Sara and prepare her for burial. A memory that will never leave my mind was the morning of Sara's funeral. My niece, Saphia, was only one year old. When walking into the lounge room, she scoped the room, hugging me first. She then made her way to Sara's mother, hugging her, followed by making a gesture to Sara's father as if she knew what had transpired. Sara and Saphia shared the same birthday, and Sara had a serious obsession with her. Upon arriving at the morgue, hundreds of my family and friends gathered to say their farewell. Sara's father had asked no-one see her except for a few people. This included my mother, my Aunty Hoda who was given the honour of washing Sara alongside her mother.

I said my final goodbye and took Sara to the mosque where we would pray on her before heading to the cemetery to lay Sara in her last resting place.

Arriving at the graveyard, Sara's father asked me to be the one to lay Sara in her grave. I asked Sara's brother Tarek to help me but he couldn't handle it, so I called upon my cousin Firass. He agreed without hesitation. Firass, one of my closest cousins, had been a part of my life for as long as I could remember. He also shared close ties with my older siblings. After putting Sara in the grave, the Sheik gave a sermon and then the tomb was closed. I sat on my knees and prayed for Sara. It was a very emotional moment. I couldn't believe she was gone. I was in denial. In two months and ten days, my life had been forever changed.

Islam's faith tells us that anyone who dies from any form of cancer will enter paradise and this was the only thing keeping me sane, knowing Sara was in a better place. After leaving the cemetery, I headed home to prepare for the three days of mourning. I remember spending a lot of time alone in bed, reflecting on old photos and reading Sara's diary. She made me promise to never to let anyone read it, and I can safely say, in the years that have passed since her death, the only eyes to have seen this diary are mine.

During the three days of mourning, many family members and friends of both Sara and me attended to show their respect. It was lovely to see how many people loved her.

A fascinating story happened on the third day of mourning. A few of Sara's childhood friends stopped by to pay their respect. I introduced myself, then one of Sara's friends said, 'We know exactly who you are. Sara has been telling us about you since she was thirteen years old, and she told us that someday she would be your wife.'

I laughed and asked, 'Really?'

'Yes,' she said. 'When she was thirteen she did an assignment based on you.'

'Of course, I remember,' I responded.

It was as if Sara had mapped out her whole life. She managed to tick every single box as well as achieve all she wanted before she passed away. The months following Sara's death were quite repetitive. I spent most of my days at the cemetery reflecting on what could have been. Although I didn't have much to report, as I had stepped away from boxing and didn't have much of social life, I would always speak to Sara. I visited Sara's parents from time to time, but it would genuinely pain me to be in Sara's home without her there. Humans are creatures of habit, so every time I visited Sara's parents, I would sit in the same spot, waiting for Sara to make her way downstairs to sit beside me. After a few visits, it became tough to keep doing this to myself.

On 11 November, I would leave Sydney for the first time since Sara's passing. A good friend, Anthony Mundine, was set to fight in Melbourne against American Charles Hatley for the WBC Silver championship. I decided I would make my way to Melbourne to support him.

CHAPTER NINETEEN
MOVING FORWARD

Leaving Sydney wasn't easy, as I still felt the need to visit the cemetery every day to see Sara. On the night of Anthony's bout against Hatley, I ran into a close friend of mine from the US, Edmond Tarverdyan, who was in Melbourne to corner for his UFC star, Ronda Rousey. We got chatting and he told me he was expecting me to be in Melbourne to support Ronda. I expressed to him I wouldn't attend, but he was adamant and even called Ronda.

She invited me to be a part of Team Rousey. Her bout would take place on the 14th, three days after Anthony's bout. I gave Ronda my word I would be there. After Mundine's shock loss, I caught the redeye flight home to visit Sara the following day at the cemetery. I took a flight back to Melbourne on the 13th to be a part of Team Rousey. I spent the day with Edmond and his team. He and I shared a room, so we had time to chat about life, losing Sara, the hospital journey and the funeral.

Edmond spoke to me about the game plan going into the fight and how Ronda would out-box Holly Holm, a former boxing world champion. As Ronda was an experienced wrestler who dominated the UFC with her unique floor game, this worried me why she would try to out-box a professional boxer like Holly. Nevertheless, Edmond was sure Ronda could do it. The morning of the 14th, everything seemed to be running smoothly. Team Rousey was supremely confident and the bookies had Ronda as a hot favourite, so we were all confident.

During the fights, I sat ringside. I had the perfect seat to watch all the action closely. After a solid undercard, it was time for the main event: Rowdy Ronda Rousey vs. Holly Holm. I was pumped. I had a redeye flight booked to be back home to be at the cemetery the following day and all I needed was Ronda to win so I could head to the airport ASAP.

The bell rang, and as Edmond had been telling me, Ronda attacked in a conventional boxing stance. Ronda attacked and Holly danced around the octagon, throwing out jabs and straight rights. I was confused. Ronda could have ended it quickly. All she had to do was take Holly to the ground and keep her there. Two minutes into the round and Ronda had landed a few significant blows. Holly responded with a few good shots of her own, showing her superior boxing skills. Towards the end of the first stanza, Holly landed some perfectly timed left hands from the southpaw stance, and the tide seemed to be shifting in Holly's favour. Round one was a good round for Holm, who had marked Ronda up. Round two was a lot like round one and saw Ronda attack while Holly walked her on to more big shots. Boom, fifty-five seconds into round two, Ronda takes a hit, she falls to the ground, and as she gets up, she's kicked in the face and knocked out. What a shock.

I couldn't believe it. The fact I was with the team would mean I needed to stay with them to make sure Ronda was okay. I got on the team bus and waited to see Ronda, but she was taken to hospital, so we followed her there. I was sick to my stomach when we arrived; the last place I wanted to see was a hospital. I sat in the waiting room with terrible thoughts going through my head. All I could think about was Sara and how much time I had spent in the waiting room as Sara wasted away. After a few hours, I summed up the courage to see Ronda. Seeing her in the hospital bed brought back more horrible memories. I said my goodbyes and rushed to the airport for my flight – I broke down as soon as I arrived home. Our home had been gutted as my older brother, Muhammad, believed we needed a change to remove the old memories and start afresh. All my belongings had been moved next door, to my brother's house, and I remember that night so clearly. I literally cried until my tears dried up.

After collecting myself, I jumped on Facebook only to see Ali Banat had been diagnosed with cancer. I couldn't believe it, another beautiful soul diagnosed with cancer. After a horrible night with barely any sleep, Adam Houda drove to my house to pick me up after learning I had been up all night crying. By far one of my closest brothers, Adam is someone I often wished was my biological brother as he had always been a phone call away. Adam took me to get some breakfast and change the mood. With tears in my eyes, I looked up and saw Ali Banet. He walked directly to me and hugged me. I was so ashamed of myself. Looking back, I had dealt with a lot, and seeing Ali left me a broken man.

During the next month, I spent a lot of time at my brother's house, as we patiently waited for our new home to be finished. I decided to go back to the gym after David Haye contacted me, asking if I would be interested in fighting on his undercard in the UK, as he was facing an

Australian opponent. I contacted Billy Hussein asking if he could visit with me as I wanted to discuss the possibility of me coming back to the gym. I explained to Billy I needed to find some happiness in my life and being back in the gym would help. We discussed the possibility of fighting on David's show, but Billy had one condition; if I didn't show him something special in the gym, he wouldn't let me fight. The other thing was my state of mind. He felt me being away from my family might not be a good idea.

A few days after catching up with Billy, I made my way back to the one place that brought me some happiness. If I'm honest, shaking off the cobwebs took some time. I felt as if I was starting my boxing career from scratch, almost as though I had never boxed a day in my life.

A week or so after the beginning of my training, we decided to use Lauren Eagles gym one night for a bit of change. After a mediocre training session, I had a minor breakdown when a conversation about Sara came up. I sat on the stairs of the ring and cried as Billy and Lauren consoled me. Billy messaged me that same night, asking me to meet him the following morning to discuss a few things.

The meeting would start the journey towards another world title opportunity. I sat with Billy at a cafe in Bankstown as he explained to me he felt best I stayed in Sydney and not go to the UK. He thought it wasn't a good idea due to my mental state. He explained we should stay home and rebuild toward another world title opportunity.

After my loss to Miura, my ranking had dropped to number thirteen in the world. I would need a few good wins to secure another opportunity. Billy came up with an idea to stay in the gym and get back in great shape while looking for potential opponents. The date he had in mind was the 26 February 2016. The venue he had in mind was The Bankstown Emporium, where I shared a fantastic night on my engagement to my late wife, Sara Salim Dib.

We left the meeting and got the ball rolling. I began to enjoy my time back in the gym around my former stablemates. My fitness was not an issue, but my timing was a little off, which took some time to get back. The opponent who would start my journey back was hardened Thai, Sukpraserd Ponpitak, who had thirteen wins against four defeats. His losses had to come against solid opposition. This fight would be no walk in the park. It was my opportunity to get back in the winner's circle and start my journey back toward another world title bout. In Sara's final message to me, she indicated she wanted me to continue striving and believing in myself, as I have done all my life.

Preparing to get back in the squared circle helped me find some real peace. It gave me something to strive towards. After all of the darkness, I was finally starting to see some light. The prep for Ponpitak was an interesting one. I was on a journey to find myself after being out of the gym for such a long time.

One day, the penny dropped. It all started with Billy's vision. It took consistency and self-belief on my end, and we were finally back to another opportunity. Thursday 25 February 2016 was the day of the weigh-in. I was so nervous; it was as if I had never been in this position before. I was pleased the show was stacked with my teammates along with my younger brother, Youssef, who appeared in his third bout as a pro. It would be the first time my brother would appear on my undercard.

The morning of the fight started the same as any other fight day. Preparing mentally, the battle could be won or lost on fight day, all of the hard work could be undone. It was essential to stick to the plan, knowing the fight was not won until the final bell rang. After a great day with my loved ones, I arrived at the venue to start preparing. My bout was scheduled for eight rounds, and I was more than ready. Moments before making my ring walk, I spoke with the media, dedicating my fight to Sara's memory. I would be taking my journey back, one round at a time and one battle at a time, on my way back to another world title opportunity.

The ring walk was an emotional one. I finally got the opportunity to put my past loss to Miura, as well as the tragedy of losing Sara, behind me to some degree. Stepping into the ring, I remember shedding a few tears. I gathered myself and stood opposite my opponent as the ring announcer read out our resumes. Firstly, my opponent, Sukpraserd Ponpitak, was hailing from Roi-et Thailand with a record of thirteen victories against four defeats and eight KOs. Then came me: thirty-nine victories against four defeats, twenty-three by way of KO. Refusing to be defined by my setbacks, I set out to get victory number forty. The bell rang and the fight was underway. I was in control and kept my opponent at bay for the majority of the bout. When the final bell rung Billy and I met in the centre of the ring and hugged it each other. It felt like a huge weight off my shoulders. Back to the ring announcer who read out the score cards: '79-73, 79-72, 79-72 ALL TO YOUR WINNER WHO MOVES ON TO HIS FORTIETH RING – BILLY "THE KID" DIB.'

During the post-fight ring interview, I was a little emotional. I thanked all those who had shown support during a very difficult time of my life.

'2015 was one of those years you don't want to remember. It was sad, but you have all helped me put something behind me that has been bothering me for some time.'

COMEBACK ACCOMPLISHED

Following my comeback victory, my world ranking moved from thirteen to eleven. It was a step in the right direction. My next bout would take place close to four months later, but a lot would occur before I stepped back in the ring again.

A lot can be said about 2016; a year that saw me back in the winner's column and the year I quite possibly made one of the biggest mistakes in my life.

Just before my bout against Ponpitak, a very close friend of mine, who I considered a brother, introduced me to a young lady. Our introduction kicked off a friendship, which brought back a little normality into my life. We would hang out often, to the dislike and disapproval of many of my friends. During this time, lots of friends and relatives in my age group were getting married and having children. A part of me felt empty and left behind but having a special friend in my life gave me hope. After a few months of hanging out, we decided to take our friendship to another level.

Again, this was met with much dislike, but I felt I was becoming somewhat of a sympathy act; it was always about how I felt. It was as though people wanted to see me in pain. It's hard to explain, but anytime anyone spoke to me they were sympathetic, and I was growing tired of it. I wanted to feel normal again, and I felt the way to do this was move on and put the past behind me. Sara was always on my mind and in my heart, but she was gone and never returning; I just needed to move forward in life.

In all truth, I was far from ready to move on, but I took the plunge. 2016 would end in disaster, but before I go deeper into this ordeal, let me take you to my next ring challenge, against an undefeated opponent who would catapult me up the IBF world rankings and back in the running for a world title opportunity.

The bout was set for 3 June 2016 against undefeated Thai, Amphol Suriyo, who boasted an impressive 17-0 sure record with thirteen KOs. The bout would be for the IBF Australasia Super Featherweight crown. My previous bout was only a few months back, so I stayed in the gym working on my plan. Once again, Billy and I were looking to put on an excellent performance, so I left no stone unturned. I took this prep extremely serious, as my opponent possessed some heavy hands, and I didn't want to make the same mistake I made in my bout with Miura, who was also heavy-handed. Once again, we would head back to Bankstown Emporium. The show would be stacked by many of my stablemates and again, my younger brother Youssef, who would appear in his fifth professional bout against a former opponent of mine, John Min, who I had knocked out in my fifth professional bout, winning the Australian Championship and taking national honours.

After a solid few months in a prep, which would include hundreds of kilometres of running, ninety-eight rounds of sparring, endless hours in the gym and a strict dieting plan to make the 130lb (58.9kg) limit, the day would finally arrive. Thursday 2 June, I was extremely professional in the lead-up, so making weight was not an issue. My opponent took to the scales first. To our surprise, he weighed in at 131.5lb. I then weighed in at 129lb. My opponent didn't even attempt to lose the weight, but I was determined to let the bout go on. If I were victorious, I would be crowned champion, but my opponent wouldn't win the title if I lost, as he failed to make the super featherweight limit. We stood face to face for the final staredown; I sized him up with victory on my mind.

CHAPTER TWENTY
FIGHT DAY

I spent the day at home with my mother, who promised she would be ringside. This meant a lot to me, as my mother never really liked watching me in the squared circle. I was one win away from being back in title contention. I was feeling fit and confident; the night couldn't come any faster.

As the night neared, I headed to the venue. I was in the zone upon arriving, as I watched my younger brother Youssef win via a second-round KO, then made my way to the change rooms to start mentally preparing for the task at hand. I started by lacing up my boxing boots to ensure I was comfortable in them. Next up was getting my hands wrapped, as usual, by Brian Wilmott.

Brian had been entrusted with protecting the tools of my trade. Watching Brian wrap my hands is like watching poetry in motion. He is master in his art. Upon finishing, Brian and I always hug. Throughout my professional career, Brian has played a much more significant role than just a cutman, Brian has been a father-figure, a brother and a friend.

As the time for battle neared, Billy gloved me up and rehearsed what we had been working on during the gruelling weeks of preparation. My family and teammates watch on, applauding my speed, power and sharpness, screaming words of encouragement. Moments before I headed out to meet my opponent for battle, my father recited a prayer; he asked the Almighty explicitly to keep both my opponent and me safe from harm. Then it's go time.

After the introductions are read, my opponent and I met in the ring's centre for last-minute instructions from the referee. I headed back to my corner, hugging Billy, Brian and Hussein. The bell is rung and the battle begins. I took complete control from the opening round, not showing my opponent any respect, as I thoroughly out-boxed and outfoxed him for most of the bout. The plan was simple, and I followed it exactly as Billy had asked of me. Ampol was a solid competitor who came to the ring with an undefeated record. His ability to recover during moments when I had hurt him was admirable, BUT after twelve solid rounds that had the crowd in attendance applauding both Ampol and me, we went to the judges' scorecards for a decision. I was confident my hand would be raised in victory. I had outworked Ampol for most of the bout. This would be evident when the scorecards were read: Kevin Hogan 118-111, Ray Wheatley 118-110 and Charlie Lucas 118-110.

By way of a unanimous points decision, the IBF Australasian Junior Lightweight Champion by way of the blue corner – Billy 'The Kid' Dib. I was officially back on the road to another world title opportunity, now rated number five in the world. It would only be a matter of time before a much-desired chance would present itself. The current IBF Champion was handy Puerto Rican, Jose Pedraza, who had made two successful defences sporting a record of twenty-one victories from twenty-one bouts with twelve KOs coming inside the distance.

What transpired following my victory over Ampol Suriyo was yet another setback which would again send my life into a whirlwind. My next bout would be 16 December 2016, but before this, I would make a mistake that would weigh me down for many years to come.

Eleven months after my late wife Sara passed away, I made a decision that haunts me to this very day. I remarried. It all seemed to happen in the blink of an eye. Six months after Sara passed away, my friendship with Sarah Shaweesh was growing at a rapid pace. Before I knew it, Sarah and I were now seeing each other three to four times a week. After a few months of hanging out, our friendship developed into a relationship, and soon we were engaged, followed by a marriage just five months after meeting and eleven months after Sara had passed away. At the time, it felt like the right thing to do, but oh how I was so wrong. After marrying Sarah Shaweesh on Sunday 24 July 2016, we set off on our honeymoon. It was from this early point I knew I had made a dreadful mistake. After the newspapers got wind I had remarried, they started trolling me. The fact some friends and relatives disapproved of my decision and also jumped on the bandwagon infuriated Sarah. She wanted me to go to war with the naysayers, but I explained to her it would only further fuel them.

I was warned my many friends and family members it was too early to move on, but I didn't want to hear it. I wanted normality in my life, but after what I was dealing with, I realised I was in for another roller-coaster ride.

When things began to spiral, I decided to take a trip to LA to spend some time with a few friends. During my time in LA, I stopped by

Riverside, California, to meet with Team Garcia; a team who had been instrumental in three of my four defeats! Working with Robert Garcia was a great experience, it allowed me to get some world-class sparring with his accomplished athletes. My time in LA was brief and before I left LA, a female friend of mine stopped by the gym to watch me train. After the session was complete, we took a few photos. After my friend posted the photo online, Sarah messaged me and asked for a divorce. She was convinced I had travelled to LA to cheat on her, which was completely absurd. I tried to explain, but I was facing an uphill battle.

Back in Sydney, I was shocked to arrive home to an empty house.

With all this turmoil going on, it was important our journey towards another championship continue. I was back in the gym preparing for my next bout which would take place on 16 December against Emilio Norfat. Once again, I would be back in action at the Bankstown Emporium function centre.

This gave me the chance to focus my energy on securing another opportunity at a world title by scoring my third win of the year. We started camp eight weeks out from my date with Emilio, who had a respectable twenty-seven victories with eight defeats. As always, our camp started smoothly. My training was on point and I was ready to secure the win, taking my record to forty-two wins with four defeats. A few weeks before wrapping up camp, Billy H and I would clash for the first time in our seven years as trainer and fighter. It was during a sparring session where Billy was praising one of the boys I was sparring with for landing a good shot. I was infuriated by everything transpiring in my life at the time and I asked Billy to be quiet. This was the first time I had disrespected Billy. Being the professional he was, he maintained the harmony in camp until our fight had passed.

Billy could see I was under a lot of pressure in my personal life and told me we would sit and speak once we had got through this fight.

Fast-forward to the night of the 16th; the fight was over quicker than the fight announcement. Emilio didn't present much of a challenge and the ref stopped the bout two minutes into the first round. I was disappointed as I had worked hard in camp and was looking forward to scoring a spectacular victory, only for the ref to step in. It was a total anticlimax and I was very disappointed I didn't get to showcase my skill set.

Nevertheless, with victory number forty-two in the bank, the anticlimax of the bout would be short-lived, as my childhood hero would make a long-awaited trip to the land down under. When I met Prince Naseem Hamed back in 2004, he promised me he would someday make the trip to Australia. It only took him twelve years, but he finally came good on his promise. He had family living in Newcastle and had made the trip to Australia to spend the festive weeks with them, as well as catching up with me. Accompanied by his wife and three boys, we had a great time. I introduced Naz to my family as well as Adam Houda. We shared a lot of time discussing what had transpired in my life over the years, as well as my divorce with Sarah Shaweesh which had become a media fiasco.

While Naseem was spending time with family in Newcastle, I took some time to visit a close friend who was somewhat of a mother-figure to me. Hajjah Nada and I were blessed to visit the holy city of Mecca in 2008, so I had developed a deep sense of respect for her. She advised me in a way which would allow me to finally heal. She spoke from a religious perspective and gave me a few tips to help me heal and move on from the many downs that had happened in my life over the recent few years. The greatest advice she shared with me was to find myself and stop trying to be like everyone else around me. She explained I was unique in my own way and all I had to do was look at all I had achieved in my life.

My meeting with Hajjah Nada allowed me to feel like the weight of the world had been taken off my shoulders.

Naz was set to leave Australia on 5 January, so I didn't have enough time to share all I wanted with him and his family. I discussed with Naz whether he felt it might be a good idea if I accompanied him back to the UK to reset and spend some time with him. As a young kid, Naz played such a pivotal part in my mindset; he was always so positive and speaking with him would leave me on such a high. I tried to speak with Naz prior to every bout; his words would always light the fire and help me chase the win. Even in defeat, Naz would always be the first to reach out and remind me that I was in the history books and winning another world championship would only further add to the legacy I had already created. I felt heading back to the UK to be in his presence could only help me heal further.

Naz agreed and I booked my flight to accompany him to Dubai for a few weeks, followed by a trip to the UK. Spending New Year's Eve with Naz and his family is a memory I will never forget. Years had passed since I first met Naz but our brotherhood had grown so much in the years since, and being in his presence was so refreshing. A few days before setting upon my journey, I spoke with Billy Hussein, letting him know I would be accompanying Naz overseas, and God willing, we would pick up where we left off after my return.

Departing Sydney never felt so good. I was excited by the chance to spend time with my childhood hero over the course of the next few months. We departed Sydney on 5 January, boarding a flight with Emirates. Naz and I would stop in Dubai for what was meant to be a few days, but would end up being just over a month.

Our time in Dubai was memorable; I met some amazing people who I now consider great friends. Naz had built an amazing name for himself during the course of his career and people in the Middle East

– and all over the world, for that matter – showed him so much love and respect. After four weeks in Dubai, we finally booked our flights to the UK. It had been a while since I last visited Naz and his family in London.

Arriving into London, Naz and I hit the ground running. We visited numerous boxing gyms, as well as one of the UK's most prominent promoters, a man who guided the majority of Prince Naseem's career, Frank Warren. We discussed the possibility of me working with Frank Warren Promotions. Although nothing ever eventuated, the trip to Dubai and the UK with Naz really helped me to heal and put the past behind me. I had been through my fair share of heartache and I was truly grateful to have the relationship and friendship I had with Naz.

After being away from home for close to three months, the time had come to depart the UK and head home to be with my family and friends. It was always hard to say goodbye to Naz and his family. I shed a few tears as I loved being in the presence of Naz. Not many people can say their childhood hero would become a brother and a confidant. Naz and I had developed a bond like no other.

Departing Heathrow Airport, I never for a moment thought it would be the last time I would see Naz for a significant time. He has been a true mentor and life-long friend, but with the pandemic and the birth of my son, I missed not being able to spend time with him face to face over the last few years, despite talking regularly on the phone.

Back in Sydney, my first priority was to meet with Billy H and tell him all about my journey, as well as work out what the plan of attack would be on our journey towards another world championship. The meeting with Billy didn't go as planned. As I mentioned earlier, Billy and I still needed to discuss and resolve what had transpired in the gym during the preparation for my last fight. After a two-hour meeting with Billy, he felt it best I explore the possibility of working with another trainer. I explained to Billy how I was sorry for my actions in the gym that morning and I was in a bad place mentally at the time. Billy explained we had achieved so much together and didn't want us to ruin our brotherhood by continuing to work together. Billy wished me all the best and said we would remain brothers as boxing was only a small part of our journey.

Our meeting ended amicably. We hugged and promised to always be brothers. I put on a brave face, but deep down I was hurting. This was the man who had taken me to the IBF crown and supported me through thick and thin.

Although I had respect for other trainers in Australia, I didn't think I could improve under any one of them, so I looked at the possibility of working with an international trainer. The only one who made sense to me was Robert Garcia. He knew me as a fighter, and I had also stopped by his gym the year before. I liked the way he ran his operation.

I reached out to Robert to see whether there was any interest from his end to work with me. Robert was welcoming but also made it very clear his top priority was his brother Mikey Garcia, as well as Abner Mares. He explained I would not always have his attention, but his assistant trainers would also be there to help. After much thought and discussion, I decided to try my luck under the guidance of the man who was responsible for coordinating three of my four losses. To make matters even more exciting, Robert would try and secure me a contract with Al Haymon, a prominent promoter in the US and a big player in the sport of boxing.

Mikey Garcia was set to face Adrian Broner at the Barclays Center in Brooklyn, New York, on 29 July and would push to get me on the undercard. Patience played a big role, but after weeks of back and forth, Mikey eventually landed me on the undercard. I arrived at Riverside to start camp with Robert on 27 June, giving me just over a month to prepare for my fight. I had stayed in shape, so it wouldn't be hard to fit right in. Mikey invited me to stay at his ranch during the prep. The experience of living with Mikey and his team was second to none. His full-time nutritionist, Frankie, was living with us, so making weight was a total breeze. The camp was professionally run and the training and sparring was quality. Training alongside Mikey was a real eye-opener, it drove me to work extremely hard to make sure I kept up with the team.

Crazy to think how a potential foe back in 2011 could become such a good friend.

My opponent for the 29 July bout was Mexico's Yardley Armenta Cruz, who had a respectable twenty-two and eight record, with twelve victories coming via KO. As always it was all business for me, as I left no stone unturned in my approach. Things were run a little differently in Robert's camp compared to the way Billy had me training back in Australia. I took everything Robert said onboard, as I tried to adapt and follow his instructions during training and sparring.

After four solid weeks of training, it was time to head to NY. Arriving a few days out from fight night, everything was on track. It was great to see the build-up surrounding Mickey's bout with Broner, and excitement was definitely in the air. I was on weight the night before the weigh-in and much of the credit should go to Frankie, with thanks for my strength and conditioning to coach Nate Arreola. On the 28th, I came to face with my opponent for the first time at the official weigh-in. It was like every other weigh-in; I made weight no problem and sized up Cruz, leaving to mentally prepare for the battle that lay ahead. Once again, I had a great team, with the support of my good friend Matt Hilliard, as well as my cousin Haissam and some friends from Sydney. Paula, Parry and Raquel all made the trip over to NY to support me.

Waking up on the morning of my fight I received some disappointing news from Robert. He told me my bout could possibly be made a swing match and if this happened, he wouldn't be able to work my corner as I would be fighting right after Mikey and Broner.

Everything Robert told me transpired. I tried to stay focused, but I was disappointed. There I was sitting in the change room with my cousin, Paula, Matt and my strength and conditioning coach Nate, with no-one on hand to wrap my hands. Suddenly, a complete stranger walked into the change room telling me he had been appointed to wrap my hands. I warmed up with Nate as Mikey and I both shared the same team. I watched Mikey's fight on the screen as I tried my best to warm up and waited for Robert Jr to come and work my corner.

I was disappointed but understood the situation Robert was in. He had warned me this could happen so there were no excuses. I needed to stay calm and focus on securing the victory.

Fifteen minutes after Mikey's bout, I made my ring walk accompanied by Robert's eldest son, Robert Garcia Jr, in my corner. I had been working with him in the gym, so it wasn't an issue. Surprisingly, there was still quite a crowd in attendance to watch the swing bouts. The introductions were given, the referee gave the final instructions, the bell was rung and the bout was on. I attacked Cruz aggressively right from the opening bell. He fired back a few shots but seemed to be more content to sit back and try to counter my aggressiveness. After a solid round one, I headed back to the corner. Jr was happy with my first round and instructed me to continue with the same approach.

Round two commenced and once again I was on the attack. Halfway through the round, Cruz rushed in with his head causing a cut to my right eyebrow, as well as suffering a minor cut to the corner of his left eye. Sensing the end was near, he opted to quit, telling the referee he couldn't see, forcing the bout to be deemed a no contest. I was infuriated; my cut was a lot worse, and I was more than willing to battle through. It was a total anticlimax, again, to have my bout with Cruz end that way. I was hoping to have a statement performance with the possibility of an IBF World Title eliminator in sight. Nevertheless, my IBF ranking would remain at three, leaving me next in line for an opportunity to fight for the crown.

It was now time to head back to Sydney, to reset and recharge before heading back to the States for my next bout. Upon arriving home, I received a text message from Robert asking me to call him once I landed in Sydney. I called Robert straight away. He wanted to discuss my previous bout, as well as what he thought about the potential of me facing Japanese-based contender, Kenichi Ogawa.

With the possibility of the fight landing in Japan, Robert expressed he would not be willing to travel to Japan. Even though he thought the bout was winnable, he didn't fancy what would follow. The current IBF Super Featherweight Champion was boxing superstar, Gervonta Tank Davis; a heavy-handed southpaw who was wreaking hell on the boxing world. So, provided the bout with Ogawa went well, Robert didn't fancy my chances against Tank.

Robert expressed his schedule wouldn't permit for him to travel, so 'maybe it was best I train with someone who didn't have such a big stable of fighters'. During the course of the following month, the landscape of the super featherweight division would change, after Gervonta Davis was stripped of the title for failing to make weight. At this point, Robert and I were still discussing the possibility of working my corner in a world title eliminator against Frenchman Guillaume Frenois, who was ranked eleven by the IBF.

Tevin Farmer, who was rated fourth with the IBF, would face fifth-ranked Kenichi Ogawa. Whoever was victorious was to face the winner of Frenois and me for the vacant world title, but Robert still wasn't able to commit to anything until he knew the schedules of both Mikey Garcia and Abner Mares.

After much discussion, Robert notified me he wouldn't able to commit and wished me all the best in my future endeavours. Although our time training together was short-lived, I learnt a lot from his teaching. In a bizarre twist, Frenois opted to pass on the eliminator, giving me more time to find a trainer to mesh with.

The IBF mandated Farmer vs. Ogawa for the vacant title on 9 December 2017, with the winner to face me the following year.

On 16 September, I attended a Save Our Sons event. It was on this night I ran into Australian boxing icon, Jeff Fenech. After a long discussion with Jeff, he invited me to join his camp with young protégé Brock Jarvis, who had an impressive eleven wins with ten KOs. I agreed. Monday 18 September would be my first session under the guidance of Jeff, alongside Brock. Training alongside a super-determined young man like Brock really helped me to get motivated. Brock was set to fight on 2 December, so he was deep into his preparation. With the IBF giving me an exemption, I was set to appear on a card headlined by Jeff Horn on 13 December.

After coming to an agreement with Horn's promoter, Dean Lonergan, I picked up the pace and was full steam into my training. A few weeks out from the bout, Jeff called to tell me I was no longer on the show but would still be paid. I had become so accustomed to the bullshit in the boxing industry, so I didn't let it bother me too much. Jeff came up with an idea to have Brock and me co-headline the show on the 2nd. I agreed and Jeff went to work on finding me a potential opponent.

It was during a short camp in Thailand that Jeff found my potential opponent, Phum Kunmat; a durable Thai with twelve wins from thirty-six outings. After wrapping up camp in Thailand, we headed back to Sydney to wrap up what was a solid camp. Both Brock and I were primed to put on good performances, but before our bouts would take place, I was introduced to my potential future. Here's how the story goes.

CHAPTER TWENTY-ONE
MEETING MY FUTURE WIFE

Upon arriving back in Sydney, it was a conversation with my sister-in-law, Chayme, that would eventually lead me to finding my future wife and mother to my baby lion, Laith Dib. On 23 November 2017, Chayme spoke to me about the potential of reintroducing me to a friend who I had met once before ten years earlier when she worked for one of my sponsors, Peter Nicholas. I couldn't quite recall who her friend was, but after seeing a few photos, agreed to the potential meet up. Chayme contacted Berry who was quick to decline a possible date, saying she was not interested. Chayme was persistent and finally got Berry to agree to catch up for a coffee on the 26th. After a short catch-up, Berry indicated she didn't want to engage in a relationship that would only waste her time. I expressed my intentions and asked her to take a chance on me. The following day, I visited Berry's mother expressing my intentions and an interest in getting to know her daughter. My future mother-in-law was very accommodating and expressed she only wanted a respectful man for her daughter. With all this positivity going on, I was looking forward to being back in the ring and putting the no contest in my previous bout behind me.

Tevin Farmer was set to face off against Ogawa for the vacant title on the 9th. I needed to be sure I had no slip-ups. I was 100% focused on the task at hand and did not overlook my opponent, giving him the respect every fighter who steps in the ring deserves.

This would be the first fight working under Jeff's tutelage, so I planned on showing a higher work rate and more aggressive side to me. The 2nd finally arrived. I had been out of the ring for over four months, but I was in prime condition running 7km every day for close to two months, so my cardiovascular was not going to be an issue. The fight went exactly as planned. I thoroughly out-boxed and outworked Kunmat, throwing close to eighty punches a round for eight rounds. Jeff was very happy with my showing, applauding my punch output and ability to take instructions well.

The following morning, I joined Berry and her family for a breakfast to celebrate my victory. It was such a happy time in my life. The Almighty does truly work in mysterious ways. I never envisioned my luck would change so soon; Berry and her family welcomed me with open arms. I was so happy to have met them all. With Berry set to take a cruise to the South Pacific on 15 December and me set to go back to Thailand for another camp on the 20th, I wanted to take advantage of the time we had after my win to get to know her. It was as though the pot had found its lid; Berry and I enjoyed many laughs and really got along well.

While my life seemed to be taking a turn for the better, Tevin Farmer lost a decision to Ogawa for the vacant IBF Super Featherweight title. Following their bout on the 9th, news began to surface that Ogawa had failed his drug test; it wasn't very clear. I was lucky to have American-based manager and agent in Sean Gibbons looking after my affairs, so I was confident it would be resolved soon. I stayed focused on my training as well as spending time with Berry.

After a few lovely weeks getting to know Berry, the time arrived to drop her off at Circular Quay to board her cruise. I had become so accustomed to having her around so a part of me was feeling very emotional; Berry and I wouldn't see each other until the 2nd of the new year, being 2018. Although communication was difficult for Berry onboard the cruise, she managed to stay in touch, sharing beautiful photos of her journey, as well as calling from time to time.

After arriving in Thailand for another short camp before New Year's, Jeff managed to secure me another hit out, this time in Thailand at the Ambassador Hotel, against a Thai local, Sayan Sirimongkhon. The IBF agreed to let me participate in the bout at my own risk. If by some chance I was to lose, I would lose my opportunity to fight for the world title. This was not likely as my opponent only had eight wins in thirty outings.

On 31 December, I faced off against Sirimongkhon in a bout that was set for eight rounds. I was happy to have the support of my relative Ahmed who made the trip from Vietnam, as well as a small Aussie contingent including Andrew Stewart, a childhood friend, as well as highly regarded criminal lawyer, Chris Murphy, and his wonderful family. They witnessed a destructive win against my overmatched southpaw opponent. I knew Sirimongkhon was not in my class and I wanted to show this by dispatching him as quickly as possible. I opened up the first round by finding my range and walking my opponent onto fast combinations. I scored effectively and managed to make it out of round one without getting hit. Early into round two, I knocked my opponent down with a barrage of shots. With Jeff screaming for the finish, I attacked relentlessly stopping my opponent halfway through round two. I was pleased to score my forty-fourth victory, maintaining my ranking with the possibility of fighting for the championship of the world in my next bout.

I celebrated New Year's with all those who were in Thailand to support me, although I wished I was in Australia with my family and Berry. The following day, I boarded a flight back to Sydney with only thing on my mind; arriving home to see Berry. I had missed her so much, it felt like a lifetime since I'd last seen her. My feelings for Berry were growing at a rapid pace; she had made such an impact in my life in such a short time. Her honesty and compassionate side really won me over.

The following months were nothing short of interesting. Ogawa failed his drug test and was stripped of the IBF Crown for testing positive, deeming his bout with Tevin a no contest. While I patiently waited for the IBF to give instructions, I stayed in the gym working hard under the guidance of Jeff, as well making the best decision in my life since marrying my late wife, Sara. I decided to ask for Berry's hand in marriage, and on 29 April 2018, Berry and I tied the knot and started our beautiful journey together.

We didn't get a chance to go away on a honeymoon as we were in deep negotiations with Di Bella Promotions in regard to my bout with Tevin Farmer.

With the help of Sean, my brother Emaid, Jeff, Mike Altamura and the man who was responsible for helping me secure the IBF featherweight crown in Australia back in 2011, Mike K, we managed to secure this mega-bout to be staged in Australia at Australian Technology Park in Eveleigh on 3 August 2018. The bout would be televised live on Fox Sports and showcase some of Australia's best up-and-coming talent.

My teammate, Brock Javis, would appear on the card, as well as rising star Tim Tszyu, who is the son of boxing legend, Kostya Tszyu.

Before the bout, a strenuous camp would take place. On 30 June, Berry and I would head to Thailand alongside Jeff and Brock, for a solid three-week camp.

Being true to myself, I left no stone unturned as I prepared to face the fleet-footed Farmer, who was riding an eighteen-fight winning streak until he lost to Ogawa in a dispute decision, later overruled and deemed a no contest. I knew the bout with Tevin would be difficult, but I felt if I could apply the same pressure Jeff would on his opponents, I might be successful. Jeff had one way of teaching; it was all about being relentless, cutting off the ring and not giving the opponent any space to move. It was hard to adapt, but I was never one to shy away from a challenge.

Running every day, as well as sparring every second day, I kept a log of all my sparring and training so I could hold myself accountable; the desire to be champion again was burning from deep within. Jeff was very supportive, making sure camp ran smoothly. Jeff's idea was to have controlled sparring, avoiding any injuries in the lead-up. The most important factor was I had the energy in the tank to see out twelve rounds if need be. Thailand was definitely a great starting point, the humidity and heat really helped with the conditioning side.

After a positive three weeks in Thailand, we headed home to continue with camp, training anywhere from two to three times daily, with only one goal in mind: to become a three-weight, two-division world champion. As a young boy, I dreamed of being champion, and here I was, fighting for the opportunity to do something not many fighters had ever done. I had wonderful support and great sponsors going into this bout; the Australian public seemed to be very excited at the prospect of having another world champion in Australian boxing.

Coming close to wrapping up what was a tremendous camp, I reached out to a former teammate and good friend, one of Australia's hidden talents, Paul 'Showtime' Fleming; a super quick, fleet-footed boxer who possessed the same silky skills Tevin Farmer had shown in his previous bouts. Paul was kind enough to lend a hand with some quality rounds of sparring.

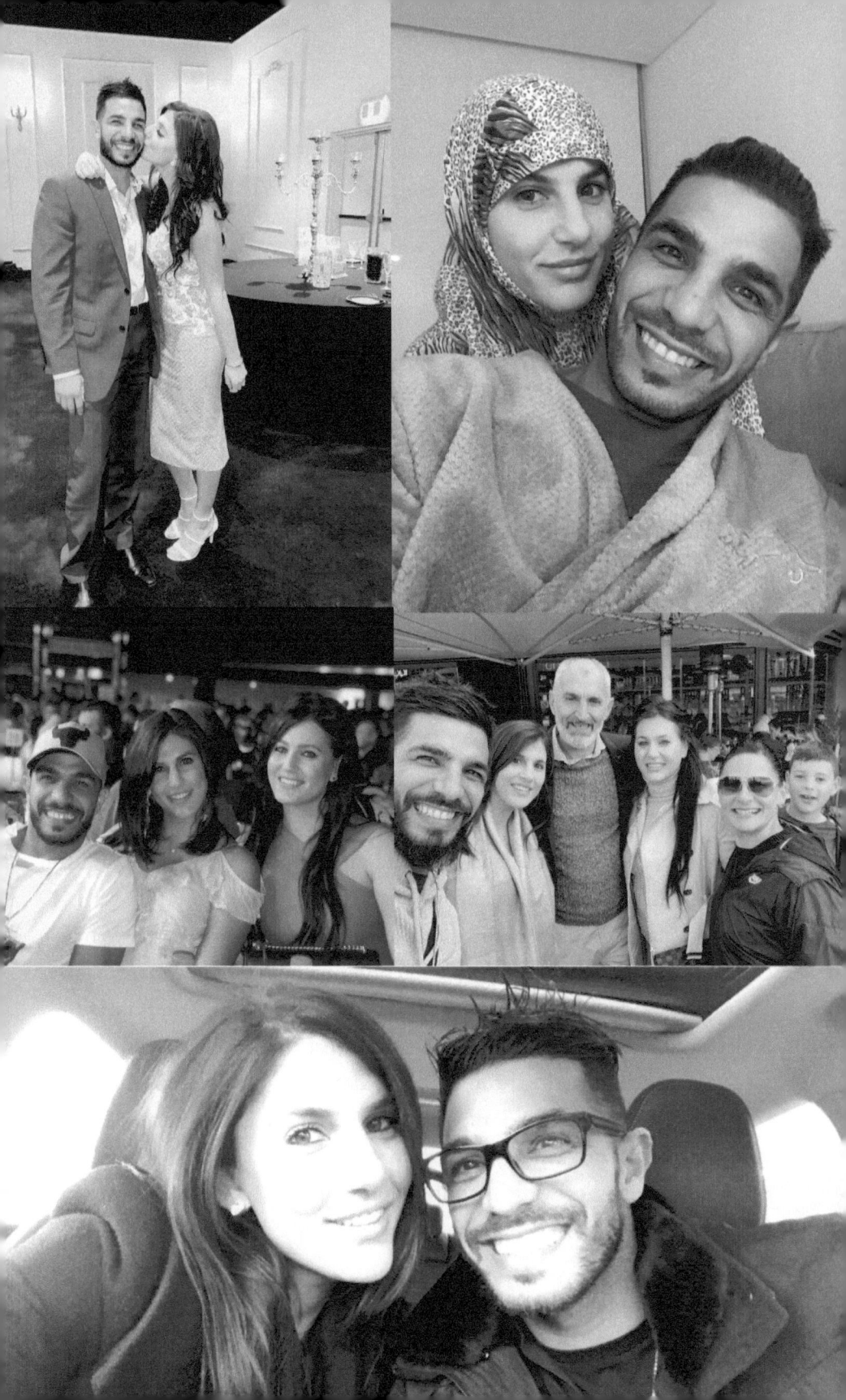

CHAPTER TWENTY-TWO
SHOWDOWN

I wrapped up my final sparring session with Paul on 27 July, just seven days out from my showdown with Tevin Farmer. The final week of training was spent sharpening up and tapering off. My weight was on point and coming off as I wanted it to. The night before the weigh-in, I went for a light 6km run to drop the remaining weight. While running, I would speak to myself, reminding myself of how hard I had been working. When I arrived home, I sat and reflected on how hard I had worked to get back to this point. Just three years earlier, I was contemplating retiring from the sport after losing to Takashi Miura in a WBC World Title bout, then losing my late wife Sara to cancer. I had managed to work my way back to the number-one position in the IBF world rankings, proving anything is possible with a vision, consistency and hard work. To my surprise I was weighting exactly 58.9kg after my run. This was all made possible by the work I had put in, remaining disciplined and focused throughout camp. After showering up, I lay down to get some sleep before the following day's much-anticipated weigh-in.

Waking up for Fajr prayers to show gratitude to the Almighty for a wonderful camp, I asked God to keep both Tevin and me safe and grant me victory if it was good for me in this life and the hereafter.

Waking up in the morning, Berry and I drove to the Ryals Hotel in Broadway where the weigh-in took place. Upon arriving at the Ryals Hotel, I was overwhelmed by all the support. My family, friends and sponsors were all on-hand. With both Tevin and me weighing in under the 130lb (58.9kg) weight limit, all that was left was the final stare-down. We stood face to face for some time. Looking deep into Tevin's eyes, I saw a man who was as determined as I was. We shook hands and went our separate ways. The next time he would see me would be in the squared circle the following evening.

I left the Ryals Hotel and headed to my father's home to be with my family. It was important I maintained routine and stayed focused. Hanging around my family the night before the fight always helped me calm my nerves as well as having my amazing friend, Matt Hilliard, by my side who had made his fourth trip down under since Sara's passing back in 2015.

We all have one friend we can truly rely on, and for me that was Matt. From the moment Matt and I met many years earlier, we really got along. We both loved the sport of boxing and had so much in common. It's safe to say, Matt is my brother and confidant. Our friendship spans way beyond boxing and I'm blessed to have him in my life.

Before the night ended, I shared a conversation with my brother Emaid who told me a lot had transpired after the weigh-in, with Tevin and his team complaining they would not be able to use the gloves they'd brought with them. The NSW boxing authority does not allow combatants to use different gloves. Tevin's choice of glove was Everlast, as was mine, but the fact he only bought a set for himself meant he would have to use the gloves my team had provided. Nevertheless, after much debacle, they agreed to use the gloves provided and the bout would go on.

The following morning. I woke up feeling motivated and grateful to be back at this point. I spent some time at Jeff's house, going over the game plan and the mindset I should take into the bout. I was quietly confident I would be successful. The fact I had overcome so much to be back at this point was a victory in itself. All that was left was to beat Tevin and capture the IBF crown. The day passed by reasonably fast; my cousin Shereef would accompany me on the drive to the venue, alongside my security guard, Peter Grant. I gave my mother and father a kiss and left for the venue, and on arriving at Technology Park, I headed to the change room to slowly get ready.

With the support of many friends and loved ones, I was pumped and ready to put my best foot forward. After performing Isha prayers, I started to prepare myself by lacing up my boxing boots, then I sat to get my hands wrapped by Brian, as Tevin's trainer Chino watched on. For some weird reason I couldn't stop my hand from shaking while Brian wrapped it. I tried my best to hide this as I didn't want Chino to think I was nervous – which to be honest, I was.

Finally, the hands were wrapped. Chino wished me luck, though of course, he didn't really mean it as he wanted Tevin to knock me spark out. I gave Brain a hug as I had always done. Jeff gloved me up and began to run me through some pad work, going over all the punches and combinations Jeff felt would work best against Tevin. As the time neared for me to make my ring walk, my father performed a beautiful prayer asking the Almighty to protect both Tevin and me. I kissed my father's hand and promised him I would do all I could to make him proud.

Accompanied by a solid team, I made my ring walk to tune of 'Hall of Fame' by The Script.

As the lyrics to the song rung through the venue, the hair on my neck and arms raised. Here was my chance to make history in my hometown. I walked up the stairs to the ring apron, raised my hands and stepped through the ropes, circling the ring. The particulars were read, and like all my previous bouts, I headed back to the corner, hugged my team and waited for the opening bell to sound.

Each and every round was closely fought. I attacked round after round as Tevin played the mediator. Even though the rounds were slipping away, I searched for a way to cut Tevin off and put a finish to the bout. His ability to be evasive was a difficult code to crack. In the ninth round, Tevin managed to put me on the canvas in what was a flash knockdown. In that moment, my whole world paused. I replayed all I had been through to get to that point, replaying Sara's death and me putting her in her grave. I looked up and saw Berry screaming for me to get up. It seemed like I had been on my knees for a lifetime. With the chance of winning on points now a distant chance, I reverted back to the style of boxing that had seen me succeed in my earlier career. Winning the last few rounds on two of the three judges' scorecards, I managed to finish the fight strong, but knew Tevin had managed to done enough to bounce back after a heartbreaking loss to a drug cheat.

Waiting for the decision to be read, I was a little emotional after my brother Emaid suggested it might be a good time to 'call it a day'. I immediately began to shed a few tears. As my family consoled me, the decision was read deeming Tevin a winner by a wide unanimous decision with scores of 119-108, 120-107 and 118-109.

Tevin was gallant and humble in victory, praising me for my relentless attack and desire to win. I took to the microphone but was quite emotional as I called it a day, bringing down the curtains on my boxing career. I left the crowd with a message, that even after everything I'd been through, I managed to find a way back, and to never give up on their dreams.

I made my way down the stairs of the ring and sobbed as I kissed my father, who told me he was so proud of me. Billy Hussein had also come along to watch the fight and support me, and I gave him a big hug and thanked him for everything he had done for me. Walking back to the change room, fans patted me on the back, thanking me for all the wonderful memories. All my family and friends applauded me as I entered the change room. After Jeff Fenech and my brother Jihad said a few words, I thanked Sean Gibbons, Jeff, my father and all those who had supported me throughout my journey.

While giving a urine sample, Tevin's attorney handed me the phone – it was Lou DiBella who was as emotional as me, congratulating me on a wonderful career. After completing my drug test, Peter dropped Berry, Youssef and me home. I spent the next few days at my parents' house recovering and spending time with Matt, who had made the trip to Australia to support me. Although the mood was a little quiet at home, there was a lot to look forward to as Berry and I were set to tour Europe for our honeymoon, just a week from the date of the fight.

The process of losing a fight never gets easy. Although I had previously suffered four defeats, I would often shed a few tears thinking about what could have been. Then I stop and think everything happens for a reason and I need to be grateful for the fact that the Almighty allowed me to achieve something not many fighters achieve – world champion status. A few days after my loss, I received a call from Prince Naz who always had the ability to lift my spirits. After a long chat, Naz left me with these final words: 'Once a champion always a champion. Remember that, Bilal. You achieved something most fighters only dream of.'

Naz always had a way with words.

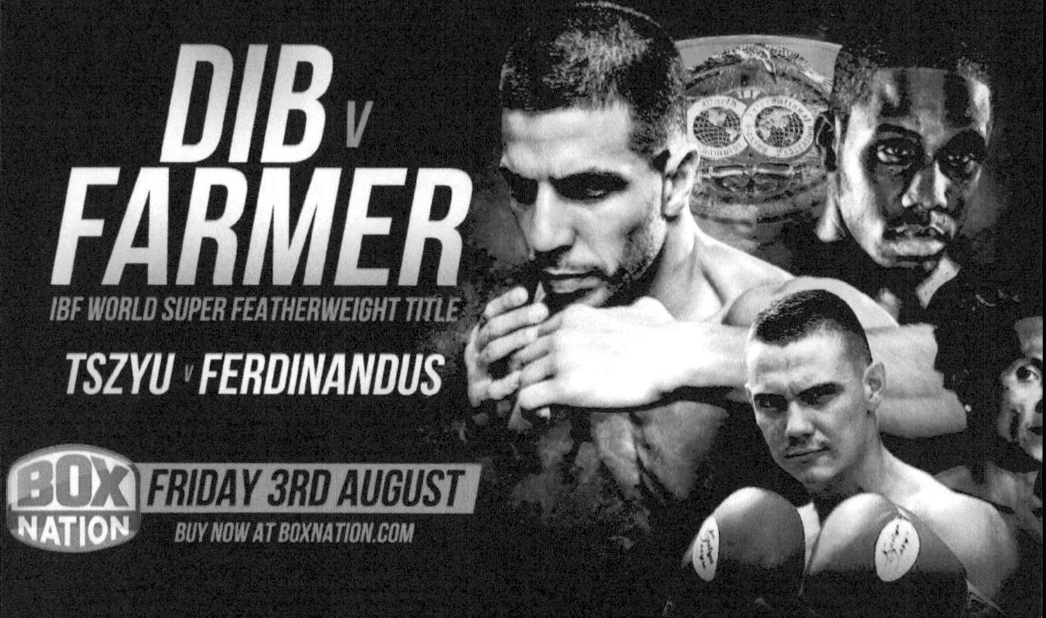
DIB v FARMER
IBF WORLD SUPER FEATHERWEIGHT TITLE
TSZYU v FERDINANDUS
BOX NATION
FRIDAY 3RD AUGUST
BUY NOW AT BOXNATION.COM

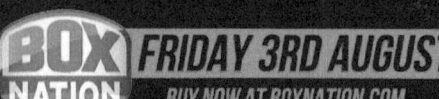

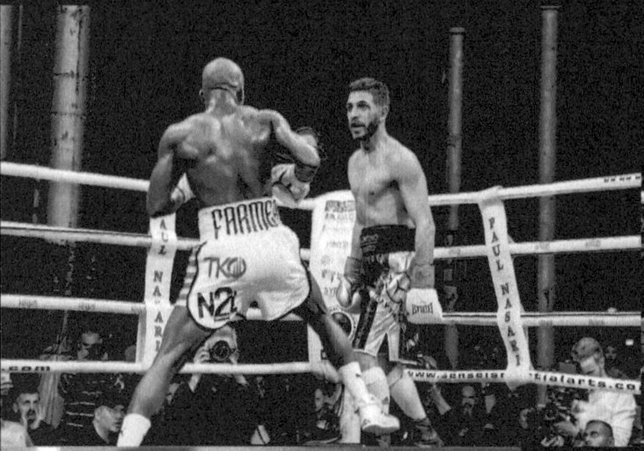
FARMER
PAUL NASARI

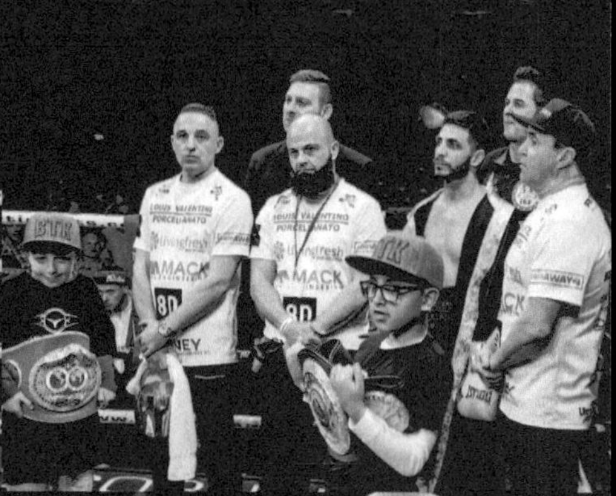

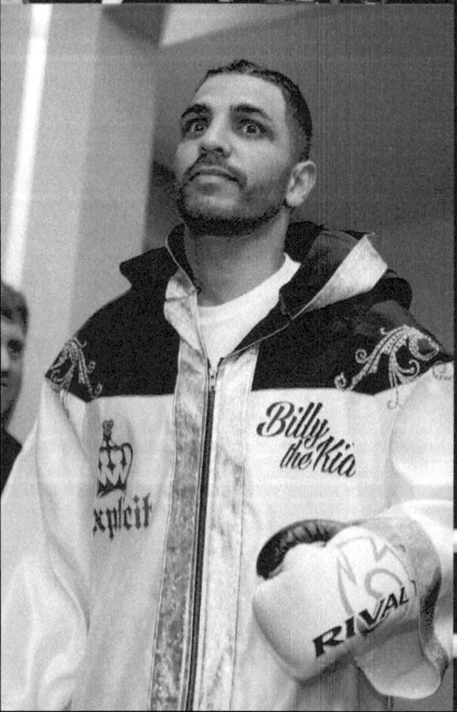
Billy the Kid
RIVAL

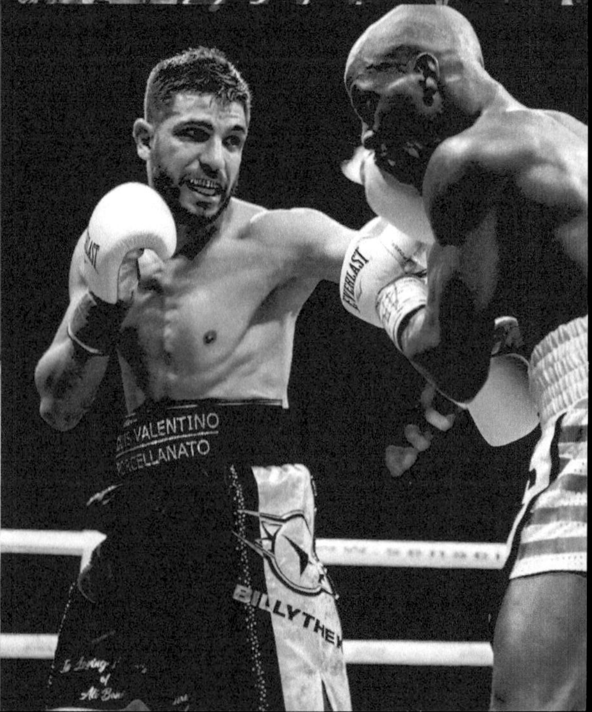
EVERLAST
PORCELLANATO

CHAPTER TWENTY-THREE
A WELCOME BACK

On 15 August, Berry and I set upon our journey to visit Dubai and Europe. We were both excited for our trip of a lifetime. Arriving in Dubai, Berry and I hit the ground running; we wanted to make the most of our time in each and every country we visited.

Turkey was our next stop. We spent an amazing week in Istanbul surrounded by beautiful Mosques, tasty food and lots of Turkish delight. We made the most of each day, doing tours and visiting museums. The Turkish hamam (Turkish baths) and listening to the call of prayer five times a day was the highlight our trip.

White buildings, blue roofs and incredible sunsets were the sights we experienced in our next destination, Santorini. We stayed in a luxurious villa overlooking the dark blue sea. Berry and I hired a quad bike and got to experience the beauty of Santorini.

Next, we landed in Italy. Rome was breathtaking. Photos don't do it justice. Walking through the streets of this spectacular city, I could only imagine what it would have looked like hundreds of years ago. We visited the Colosseum and walked through history. I was so intrigued by the architecture. We did tours around the whole city during our time in Rome, exploring the past and present – each day was a history lesson.

Up and away again, we were on a flight to Malaga, Spain. I remember arriving there really early in the morning. Once we settled in our room, we freshened up and headed out for lunch. Malaga was very chill. We walked along the ports and visited the beach daily.

Barcelona was next on the list. We were there for five days, so got to explore the city and visit all the main attractions. During our stay there, Berry started feeling unwell and wasn't herself. It was 7am and I heard Berry screaming out, 'Billy, Billy!' I woke up and ran to see what was going on.

She was holding a pregnancy test stick. 'I'm pregnant,' she said. I jumped for joy. I was so happy. The sadness I had felt after my loss to Tevin disappeared in that moment. We hugged each other and began to cry.

We made a few phone calls to our families back home and told them the good news. They were all so excited and happy for us.

Life after boxing was starting and as sad as I was, I knew something better than any world title belt was coming my way.

Paris was our final destination. The next four days was all about the baby and what we wanted to do when we got back home. Berry was ready to go home. She had been feeling ill the whole time but didn't know she was pregnant until now. It all made sense now.

Upon arriving in Paris, we found out my beloved Aunty Hoda and Uncle Sam were also there. We were so excited to see family from home. It had been five weeks, and we were getting homesick.

That night, we went out for coffee with my aunty and uncle. We shared with them the great news about Berry's pregnancy. They were delighted.

We planned to meet with them the next day to explore the beautiful city of Paris. We started at Notre Dame, visited the Eiffel Tower, then made our way to the Arc de Triomphe and the classy street of the Champs-Élysées. We were making sure we didn't miss out on anything. We enjoyed a lovely lunch together and continued exploring Paris by boat, soaking in every minute of this amazing city.

The day finally arrived; after five weeks away, we were making our way back home. Europe was an amazing experience for both Berry and me, we enjoyed every bit of it and captured hundreds of photos to add to our memory book.

This trip also brought Berry and me closer together.

On arriving home, reality hit. I had left the sport of boxing with no exit strategy. The following months after our honeymoon were quite challenging. The excitement of being a soon-to-be father was all I was looking forward to. But I had been around the sport of boxing my whole life; it was all I knew. I had gone from living a structured life, boxing, running and living and eating clean. Our honeymoon was great but now being home, I felt lost. I tried to hide it from Berry as I didn't want her to worry about me during her pregnancy.

A part of me felt as though everything would fall into place. I never planned for life after boxing; I figured I'd go with the flow and let life take its path. This simply didn't work. I needed to find something to fill the void. A part of me felt guilty but I really needed to stop worrying about me and start directing my energy towards Berry and her pregnancy, as there was so much to look forward to.

I started to settle into the excitement of being a soon-to-be father, until Berry began to experience complications. On 9 October at 4:55am, Berry screamed for help. I woke up and rushed to the bathroom only to find Berry in some serious pain. Not knowing what was going on, I called 000 stressing my wife was 'not in a good way'. After arriving at the hospital and running a few tests, the doctors explained Berry had unfortunately experienced a miscarriage. We were both devastated but always had faith that the Almighty had a better plan for us both.

The following weeks were filled with much sadness. Even though we accepted the Almighty's plan for us both, it was still a bitter pill to swallow. Deep down I was hurting; never did I think I would get to the point in life where I simply had nothing to do.

Berry and I decided another getaway was a good idea. This time our destination was Bali. Arriving on 9 December, our time in Bali was memorable. Berry and I left no stone unturned doing anything and everything from surfing to theme parks. I even visited a boxing gym. The trainer asked if id ever boxed. I said, 'No ... but I'd like to try!' LOL. I asked if I could spar.

His response was, 'But you don't have mouthguard.'

'No problem,' I said.

He lent me some gloves and I jumped in the ring. He put a young Balinese pro in with me. The kid threw a few shots and I made him miss, then opened up on him. The trainer was shocked. 'Are you sure you've never boxed before?' I smiled and told him who I was. He then recognised me and showed me so much love and respect.

After ten beautiful days in Bali, it was time to head back to Sydney. Walking into the gym in Bali reignited my spark. I discussed with Berry that I'd like to get back into the gym and 'see how I go'. When we arrived back in Sydney, I contacted Billy Hussein asking if we could get together. Billy always made time for me, so a catch-up was a given.

A few days later, I popped into the gym to speak with Billy; he had no idea what I wanted to talk about. I explained to him how the past few months had been really difficult and I was a little lost without the sport of boxing. I expressed my interest in wanting to come back and train. He was so accommodating, telling me the gym was mine and the doors would always be open to me. I wasn't sure if I wanted to fight again, but I wanted to come back and train with the team and simply see how it unfolded.

With another getaway booked, I told Billy I would come back in the New Year and start training. With the New Year underway, Berry and I were set to join my brother Emaid and his family along with some friends on a trip to the Queensland and Byron Bay.

Upon our return, I immediately got back into training. It was good to be back in the gym doing what I loved most. Being in the gym bought me so much happiness; from sparring to everyday training, I was really starting to enjoy myself again.

With Billy set to promote a show in the coming months, I quietly started to prepare myself for a return to the squared circle. Once a date was firmed up, I sat with Billy and discussed the possibility of making my return to the sport. Billy was happy to once again train and promote me, but wanted the blessing of my father and brother, Emaid. Of course, my family would have loved for me to stay retired but wanted to see me happy, so they gave Billy the green light and my return was set for 26 April 2019.

CHAPTER TWENTY-FOUR
BERRY ONCE AGAIN FALLS PREGNANT

While life was starting to feel good again, it was just about to get a whole lot better. Berry notified me she was experiencing some nauseousness and tiredness, so she decided to take a pregnancy test in the early hours of 26 March while I was asleep. Berry screamed with joy, 'Billy … Billy … wake up!' I rushed to the bathroom and saw Berry holding up the pregnancy test, showing two lines, meaning Berry was pregnant once again. I raised my hands as though I had just won the championship of the world.

With a date in sight, my excitement was on overdrive. With Berry now pregnant, I had so much to fight for. Billy H went to work on finding a credible opponent; an experienced Thai who had an impressive twenty-one wins with only two losses. I was happy to be facing an opponent of his calibre. Days out from the bout, I learnt from Billy that my opponent's visa had not been cleared and he wouldn't be in Australia in time for the fight. Billy did everything he could to find a credible replacement, but we were left scrambling. It was vital that I fight, as many fans had purchased tickets to see me compete. In a last-minute move, Billy matched me with Surachet Tongmala, another Thai opponent with an unimpressive seven wins and eleven losses.

Happy to make my return, I dispatched my over-matched opponent, knocking him out as round one was coming to an end. Even though my opponent was over-matched, waking up the following morning as a winner was a wonderful feeling, one I still find hard to explain. Even though I was a little disappointed with my opponent, I was happy to be back in the winning circle.

The faith of Islam tells us that with news of a child, the Almighty will send unexpected wealth; and for me, it was just about to happen. A month after my most recent win, I received a call on 1 June from long-time friend, former two-time world champion, Amir Khan. He offered me the opportunity to appear on his undercard, on a show to be promoted in Saudi Arabia. This would be the first time boxing would be promoted in the Arab world, and to be a part of it would be historical. Of course, I accepted Amir's offer. The only thing that worried me was the fact Amir could only offer me a bout of four rounds. I hadn't fought in a four-round bout since making my professional debut back in 2004. I pleaded with Amir for a few more rounds, but his hands were tied and the offer was four rounds or no fight at all. In fairness, the money I was being offered was more than some champions were getting paid in world title fights, so I bit my tongue and took what was on offer.

I contacted Billy and Emaid to notify them of the news. I explained to Billy that we could have an opponent of our choice. He wasn't impressed we would only appear in a four-round bout, but understood the offer was too good to decline. After a few days of searching for an opponent, Indonesian Isack Junior was presented to me as a potential opponent. With a respectable twenty-five wins from thirty-nine outings, with three draws, Isack was perfect. I contacted Amir's team notifying them of my opponent. He was approved and the SBL promotional company went to work on getting our visas sorted so we could travel.

The names of my team would be needed in advance, as we all required a visa to enter the Holy Land. With Billy unsure whether he could make the trip, his brother Hussein would accompany me. I also had the option of bringing a third member and with both Emaid and Brian busy, I chose to take my best friend, Morad.

With a month to prepare, Billy and I got to work. The game plan for this bout would be a simple one. Isack was a decent scrapper, but my skills far outweighed his. Four-round bouts could be dangerous, but I was smart enough to out-box Isack and avoid any serious damage.

With the promotion nearing and our visas approved, we would head to Saudi Arabia ten days out from the bout, assuring there would be no jet lag. It wasn't long before our preparations to leave when I received a call on 19 June from the SBL promoter Bill Dosanjh, notifying me he was on his way to Australia and needed to meet with me. I told him he was crazy as I would be in Saudi in the coming week and we could speak then. But he was adamant we meet urgently, so I agreed.

The following day, at 2pm, I met with Bill. I was very curious to see why he had flown all the way to Australia to see me. We had arranged to meet in the restaurant at the Sheraton in Hyde Park. I had met him before, so I knew exactly who I was looking for. Once I spotted Bill, I greeted him and we sat down to talk. He filled me in on all the ins and outs of the current promotion, future plans and how he wanted me involved, to some extent. It all sounded very exciting, but it didn't add up why he had flown all the way to Australia to talk to me about these potential future plans. Bill then asked whether I'd really lost over a million dollars in the deal with 50 Cent. 'Yes it's true,' I responded, 'but it's in the past now.' I explained to Bill about when Sara was in hospital and the doctors had revealed she wasn't going to make it. I told him what Sara's father had told the doctors that he would pay anything to save his daughter. The doctor's response was that money couldn't help. I explained to Bill how I had decided to part ways with the money, right then and there. Moments later, Bill asked if I'd like to go for a walk. He asked me to switch off my phone. Alarm bells were ringing in my head. 'Why?' I asked. He explained he needed to discuss something private and wanted me to concentrate on what he was about to tell me. I switched the phone off and gave him my full attention.

The chat started negatively; the first thing Bill had to say was that the show was going to be cancelled. I couldn't believe I'd been sitting with this man for the last two hours, listening to him ramble on about the plans for the show, all the while knowing it would be cancelled. He explained Amir's opponent had been injured and they were struggling to find a replacement. I told Bill there would be plenty of opponents who would put their hand up to fight Amir. His response was how it would be very difficult to get a visa this close to the event. Still not catching the drift, Bill once again repeated, 'You need a visa to get into Saudi Arabia.' I responded by saying, again, that anyone would jump at the opportunity. 'Would you?' he asked.

'Me? Are you crazy? I'm a super featherweight at best. Amir is a welterweight, probably coming down from middleweight. It would be madness for me to fight him.'

Bill then said, 'What if I could replace the money you lost on the 50 Cent deal?' I couldn't believe what he was saying.

'If you send me a contract tonight, you have a deal. But I have a few conditions.'

'Sure,' Bill responded.

'I want two business class flights. Also, when I beat Amir, you will negotiate a better deal for me. And on the chance Amir beats me, I get an opportunity to appear on his next undercard for a minimum of US$250,000. Do you accept?'

Bill's answer was, 'Okay, no problem. But you know you won't win; Amir is simply too big for you.'

'Let me worry about that,' I told him.

Bill and I shook hands. He asked me to keep it to myself and not announce anything until he gave me the green light.

Immediately after leaving Bill, I got in the car and called my wife, Berry. She thought it was a joke. I explained it was a life-changing opportunity and with the birth of our child later in the year, our lives would be so much more comfortable.

Berry didn't really care about the money. She was more interested in my safety and was not super keen on seeing me face Amir at such a weight deficit. I explained I would be okay and was going to go through with it. With Berry now four months into her pregnancy, she wouldn't be permitted to travel, so I would need to leave her behind, but I knew this was an opportunity to better our lives and give our child a better life.

After getting off the phone with Berry, I contacted my mother. Years earlier she had told me the money I had lost on the 50 Cent deal would somehow find its way back to me. I told Mum of the opportunity presented to me and also reminded her of what she'd told me all those years ago. 'Mum, God is good. The money you said would find its way back to me, just did. I'm fighting Amir Khan.'

My mum's response was so cute. 'But aren't you and Amir friends?' she asked.

I laughed and said, 'Yes, but it's okay, Mum – we will still be friends.'

I couldn't believe this was happening; from fighting on the undercard, to now being the main event against Amir Khan. Now to tell Billy Hussein! I arrived at training at 5pm. Upon seeing Billy, I asked if we could have a private chat in the karate room.

'Billy, what do you think it would be worth if I was to fight Amir Khan?'

'What are you talking about? That's ridiculous,' he responded.

'I'm just asking,' I replied. Billy mentioned the sum of $300,000.

'So, Billy … It turns out Amir Khan's opponent has injured himself and they've asked me to step in.' I told Billy the offer and how it was an opportunity of a lifetime. Billy agreed, and we were all guns blazing. We were now left with the hard task of trying to secure Billy a visa with just three weeks left until fight day. I contacted a family friend to see if he could help speed up the process.

While all this was happening, I would share the joy of finding out my wife and I would be blessed with a baby boy. This gave me so much more motivation; our gender reveal was one I will never forget. Berry's idea was to associate boxing in our reveal – the picture tells the story. The joy I felt can't be explained. A boy … a little me. The joy brought tears to my eyes as I hugged Berry. With so much to fight for, I picked up the pace knowing there wasn't much time left until I would depart for Saudi Arabia.

With Billy's visa now in the works, we got to work. We reached out to long-time friend and brother in Islam, Anthony Mundine, to see if he could help me with some sparring. As always, Choc was all class and happy to help. We also had the help of gym mates Kanaan Eletri and undefeated junior middleweight pro Alex Hanan. Amir Khan was extremely fast and big, so I needed to see that kind of speed and size, hence the reason we reached out to Choc.

Now I would be facing Amir in the main event, I would need to make my way to Saudi Arabia a lot earlier, due to media commitments, meaning I would have less than ten days to cram in as much sparring and training in with Billy as I could. Billy's visa was taking longer than projected and as my departure date neared and Billy's visa still had not been passed, we made arrangements for my training once I arrived in Saudi. Close friend of mine, Nettles Nasser, was living and training kids in Saudi Arabia. He was an experienced trainer, and Billy and I agreed he was the right man for the job.

On 1 July, Morad and I would set upon our journey to Saudi, travelling in the comfort of business class. Our flights were enjoyable. I had travelled business class many times, but this time it was different. For the first time in my career, I could enjoy the food and drink on my way, as making weight would not be an issue with me fighting in the welterweight division; three weight divisions higher than my usual super featherweight.

After a long but enjoyable flight, Panda and I arrived in Saudi Arabia. The team at SBL promotions transported us to our hotel where we hit the ground running – literally. I got changed into some training clothes and hit the gym to shake off the jet lag, putting in a 6km run. A few hours later, Nettles met us at the boxing gym to put some work in.

The game plan was simple; be smart and use angles and speed to try and keep Amir off. I was definitely up against it as Amir was naturally a much bigger man. I was a little concerned. The fact I was in Saudi Arabia, getting ready to face my biggest test without my head trainer, really bothered me. I had been assured Billy would arrive on 5 July, giving me exactly seven days with Billy until the fight.

The greatest blessing for Morad and me was the opportunity we were given to perform Umrah in the holy city of Mecca. On 4 July, I decided to take a day off training to perform Umrah. In 2008, I was blessed with the opportunity to make Hajj and now I would be blessed with the opportunity to make Umrah with my best friend Morad. To say we were given the royal treatment would be an understatement; Morad and I were blessed with the opportunity to pray right in front of the Kaaba. Driving home, we were so pumped. It is an honour and a blessing to visit the holy city of Mecca. Allah had chosen us, and we felt so blessed.

The following morning, Billy arrived in Saudi Arabia. I was so happy. I felt comfort in Billy's presence, knowing he was by my side. With six days until the weigh-in, we stayed on path, training twice daily. We would train in the morning then head out for the day before going back to the gym for our second session of the day. A few days after Billy's arrival, we decided to change hotels as Billy felt uncomfortable with the surroundings. With the help of Nettles, we moved our belongings to a five-star hotel, and that same night, I sparred for the last time, four days out from my bout with Amir.

The lead-up to the bout was nothing short of exciting. For the first time in my career, I truly felt like a superstar. Billboards with images of Amir and me were plastered all over Jeddah, and a boxing ring had been assembled at the main shopping centre for the public to watch us during our media sessions. Superstars from the world of boxing, UFC and hip-hop would be in attendance to watch us during our media workouts.

The day before the bout, Amir and I would face-off at the final press conference. When called to podium, I started by thanking the Almighty for this amazing opportunity. I thanked Amir and his team as well as my team, Billy Hussein, Morad and Nettles, for the amazing support. I mentioned this was a great opportunity, and nothing was expected from me as Amir was a much bigger man. I also mentioned that when you expect nothing, you get everything. I was here to win and would do everything in my power to win this fight. After a few words from Amir where he showed a lot of respect, we stood up to 'stare down' for the media in attendance. The size difference was evident, but I would not be deterred.

We shared a few laughs with Paulie Malignaggi, before heading back to the hotel for our final pad work session before the following day's official weigh-in, which was set to take place at 5pm in front of a live crowd at the Red Sea Mall. This is where all the controversy began to take place. I had no issues making the welterweight limit of 147lb, in fact I was having issues putting on weight, where Amir seemed to be struggling to get to the 147lb (66.6kg) limit.

I received a call from Panda notifying me the weigh-in had been moved from 5pm to 9am. This just proved Amir was struggling to make the weight. I was a little upset by this as Amir would now have close to forty-eight hours to replenish. I voiced my concern about this as I was moving up three weight divisions to face Khan at welterweight. Amir turned up to the weigh-in looking completely dry. I was first to the scales coming in at a heavy 145lb (65.7kg), while Amir weighed 146.4lb. To top things off, when it came to selecting gloves for our bout, Khan and his team opted to use 8oz Grant gloves. I felt this was a little unfair, as I would be giving away loads of weight once Amir had hydrated. We argued we should use 10oz gloves, but the excuse was there were no other gloves available.

I would once again see Khan at the public weigh-in at Red Sea Mall, with a huge crowd in attendance, including boxing legends Lennox Lewis, Paulie Mallignaggi and UFC greats Chuck Liddell and Israel Adesanya. The atmosphere was electric. To say I was in shock when I saw Amir would be an understatement. Earlier that morning, he looked as though he was going to faint. Now, he looked about 10kg heavier. We faced off once again and this time the size difference was very evident. I took a deep breath and remember thinking, *My goodness, he is a big welterweight.*

Off to the hotel to get some rest before the big day. Looking back, I remember feeling completely relaxed. I spent a few hours on the phone with Berry and my brother Emaid who were both so proud of me for taking this opportunity. There was no pressure on me. Nothing was expected of me as Amir was a much bigger man, but I have always had the heart of a lion and always been determined to succeed, giving it my all in my quest for victory.

On fight day I woke up completely relaxed and focused. This task was nothing short of huge, but I zoned in and focused. A trip to the barbers to get a trim as well as burning some time with Billy, Morad and Nettles, we spent the day having fun. Before I knew it, it was time to pack my things and head to the venue. Picked up by a private car, we headed to the King Abdullah Sports City arena in Jeddah.

As I had mentioned earlier, I have never been made to feel like such a superstar. The stadium doors had pictures of Amir and me facing off, as well as life-size billboards of us around the stadium. Rap stars Rick Ross and Tyga were also in the building, entertaining the massive crowd in attendance. After checking out my change room and getting comfortable, the WBC commission reweighed me, and to my surprise, I had lost weight since the morning's weigh-in. On the other hand, Amir would be entering at a whooping 75kg, exactly 10kg heavier than me. After weighing in, I took a walk outside to soak in the atmosphere; what a feeling it was. Here I was, fighting in Saudi Arabia as the main event, against established welterweight star, Amir Khan. This was huge.

With hours to burn, I headed back to my change room to watch the stacked undercard featuring former champion, Samuel Peter, as well as many upcoming stars. Nettles started wrapping my hands around 10:30pm, giving me ample time to warm up, as I wasn't scheduled to be in the ring until midnight.

With Amir being so much bigger, it was important I use my feet to stay out of harm's way. With Khan coming off a loss to pound-for-pound star, Terence Crawford, I was sure he would be looking to make a statement against me, especially as I was a much smaller man.

After warming up, the time had finally come for me to make my entrance to the squared circle. Making my ring walk, rap star Rick Ross offered to walk me out, but I opted to give it a miss, using a song of my choice – 'Ambition' by Wale. With a huge crowd in attendance, the love they showed me was inspiring; I was pumped.

Next up was Amir, accompanied by Tyga and his entourage. Once the particulars were read, we came face to face for the final instructions. Billy's final words to me were stay low and don't stand in front of him. I gave Morad and Billy a hug, and the fight was a go.

As instructed by Billy, I kept my distance, occasionally throwing out a jab. Khan showed glimpses of speed, but my movement made it difficult for him to pin me down. With round one coming to a close, I had made it further than many people had expected. Billy instructed me to keep it simple and not gamble too much. A minute into round two, I lunged at Khan with a left hook, only to be countered by his own left which left me seated on my bum. I took a knee and rose to my feet at the count of eight. Completely clear in the head, I spent the remainder of the round avoiding any engagement with the bigger man.

Round three was much better as I avoided most of Amir's attacks as well as landing many blows of my own. It was the following round that saw the bout come to an end. I had made it a lot further than many had expected. This bout reminded me of Khan vs. Canelo in regard to the size difference. The bout came to end at 2:07 of round four, after Amir attacked with a flurry of punches which ended with him nailing me with his forearm, flooring me once again. I rose to me knee, only to notice Billy had thrown in the towel.

I was a little disappointed, but Billy was there to protect me, so I didn't complain. This was the biggest payday I had received in my career, and I was appreciative for the opportunity. Amir was all class, in giving me credit for showing so much heart in moving up to welterweight to face him.

This was a loss that would not hurt me in any way. WBC president Mauricio Sulaiman was so proud of the heart I showed, he offered to put me in position to fight for the WBC silver title in my natural weight.

With so much to look forward to, I made my flight home to be with my wife, who was due to give birth in late November/early December. The opportunity against Amir was amazing, but the payday was life-changing, and I was so happy I finally got the money I felt I always deserved. Through faith and hope, the Almighty had delivered me the money I had lost in the deal with 50 Cent.

The next few months were nothing short of amazing. The blessing of watching my baby boy grow in his mum's tummy was beautiful. On 20 November, Berry and I attended the clinic for a check-up only to be notified the baby was in distress and Berry would need to be induced. We rushed home, packed our bags and made our way to the Royal Prince Alfred Hospital, where Berry would give birth the following day. The excitement was real; I contacted my mother as well as Berry's siblings to let them all know of the good news. Berry's sister, Lina, as well as my mother, would be on hand to witness this beautiful miracle called birth.

CHAPTER TWENTY-FIVE
THE FARM

Let me wind it back and tell you about Uncle Angelo 'the Greek' Sarandopoulos. I met Angelo just before I fought Tevin Farmer in 2018. He was there to watch me perform that night, coming with his son-in-law, Mohammad, who is also my wife's brother. Not long after my defeat to Farmer, I had several phone conversations with Angelo. We stayed in contact regularly and formed a beautiful friendship; I know he is one person I can count on with anything in this life. Angelo began to mentor me and became somewhat of a father-figure, helping guide me through many personal and life decisions. He played a major role in helping me physically and mentally, helping to reignite the fire in my belly that I felt had been doused following the disappointing loss to Farmer. He explained that he'd seen enough from me in that performance to know there was still a spark and he could help bring out the best in me again.

Having competed for many years as a long-distance runner at a very high level and eventually going on to become a successful personal trainer and businessman in the corporate world, Angelo knew what it took to progress to new levels in life. We decided Angelo would take over all my running and sprints training and we went to work soon after. My running times and technique improved dramatically. This played a major role in my fitness, but it was mentally where I was improving the most. Our work together had me feeling young again and I was confident I still had enough in the tank to compete at the world level.

The birth of my son led to a sense of urgency towards my obligations as a man, as a father and as a husband. Watching my wife give birth to this little human being gave me a new-found respect, not just for Berry, but for women in general. This was a new beginning for Berry and me as we became parents for the very first time. Berry and I decided to name him Laith, which is an Arabic term for a baby lion. Laith brought so much love, pride and joy into our lives, but this is not to say that he didn't bring his challenges with him.

During this time, I was preparing for a fight against an opponent named Van Thao Tran, an undefeated boxer from Vietnam. This fight was an important one for me, as it marked my first fight back following my loss to Amir Khan. It was an opportunity for me to work my way back into the world rankings against a well-credentialed fighter, but the stresses of being a new father were starting to get to me. As an athlete, training is important, but sleep is just as essential for your recovery. With Laith being so unsettled at home and dealing with what we believed to be colic, my sleep each night was continuously disrupted and some nights, non-existent. Regardless, I had to put it behind me and focus on the difficult task at hand, giving a fighter who has never known how to lose, his first loss as a professional.

Fast-forward to 21 December, the morning of the fight with Van Tran. Berry came to me and told me she didn't want Laith to go to the fight night which was pretty dampening for me. I was so excited to have Laith there at one of my fights for the very first time but could understand the reasoning behind it. I left for the venue that night, not expecting Laith to be there.

Upon arriving at the venue, I started to mentally prepare myself for battle and went through my regular pre-fight motions. Just as I was about to put my phone away until after the fight, I received a call from Berry where she told me both her and Laith would be attending. This truly gave me a burst of energy and a feeling 'there was not a way in the world I could lose tonight'. When Berry arrived with Laith at my change room, I could not help but tear up at the sight of my son, knowing he was by my side before going out to war.

The match against Van Tran proved to be a tough one. He was a willing and worthy opponent. He was obviously hungry, not just to keep his undefeated record intact, but also to add a former two-time world champion to his list of scalps. As determined and hungry as he was, though, I had something bigger to fight for and he was watching me ringside for the very first time. I refused to let Laith down. Each time Van Tran started to gain some momentum, I made sure I snatched it back, scoring with some quick flurries and counter shots. As the fight progressed, I found I could do my best work when I had him backed up on the ropes, and I set out to do that for the rest of the fight. We went the full distance of ten rounds and I was pronounced the WBC Australasian Super Featherweight Champion after picking up a convincing unanimous decision. As soon as the fight was done, I felt the need to have Laith with me so I brought both him and Berry up to the ring. The joy of victory is always sweet, but this time was different. The sense of pride I had in lifting Laith high in the ring is indescribable. It was something I had envisioned for a long time, even as a youngster watching former greats do the same with their own children.

In the not-too-distant future, my life would once again be changed forever. My father, brothers and I were invited to spend some time at the farm of a great family friend of ours, Danny Abdallah. I was reluctant to go at the time because it would be the first time I would be leaving Berry and Laith for a few days. My brothers convinced me it would be a good idea to go and an opportunity to spend some time with Danny, who had gone through tragedy just a few months earlier. Danny and his beloved wife Laila became known to the world as the parents who lost three of their beautiful children and their niece in a tragic car accident.

Driving to the farm with my brother Emaid, we had a deep conversation about what I wanted to do with my life. I revealed to him that I would love the opportunity to inspire the world with my story and the events of my life. Emaid then mentioned that I should make myself available for some keynote speaking and put it out on my social media platforms. The first night at the farm, my family and I were joined in the main hall with several friends and family of Danny's, who were also spending time at the farm for the weekend. It is there I had a fateful meeting with someone who would help change my life. With twenty to thirty people gathered around as I shared stories of my boxing career and of the celebrities I had spent time with, one man's actions stood out. That man, who I later came to know to be Sid, told someone else who was interrupting my stories on a few occasions to, 'Shut the fuck up and let him finish!' This took me aback as I didn't know Sid, yet he was so engaged in my stories he wouldn't allow someone to cut me off. To say that it left a lasting impression would be an understatement.

As the night wound down and everyone was readying themselves for bed, Sid came to me and introduced himself as Danny's personal life coach, saying, 'Do you know that you're worth anywhere between $5-10 million, all day, every day?' I didn't understand what he was saying, thinking he was insinuating my 'net worth' to be $5-10 million. I told him I was worth nowhere near that amount to which he replied, 'Yes, you are, you just don't know it yet.'

Sid explained to me that he had mentored many people who had gone on to have success in the public speaking circuit. That blew me away, considering I had just spoken to Emaid about the same thing. 'I want you to let that manifest in your mind and we'll talk about it in the morning,' Sid said. I couldn't sleep as I pondered upon what he'd told me. All I could think about was what Sid said and had an overwhelming feeling about how the next chapter of my life was unfolding.

The following week, I met with Sid at breakfast, and he made me a proposal to mentor and support me through the next few chapters of my life. He promised to help improve my keynote speaking and was adamant my personal experiences were enough to inspire millions of people around the world, saying all I needed was the right platform to tell my story. This would be where our focus would turn to over the next few years.

With Sid, Angelo, my brother Emaid and marketing genius, Atal Hakikat, I was now armed with an amazing group of people around me to help guide me in setting up the next phase of my life. I felt I was covered from all angles and everything in my life was progressing in a positive direction. I had a clear sense of direction and my motivation to succeed for my wife, Berry and young son, Laith was sky-high. On the boxing front, my victory over Van Thao Tran had placed me back in the world ratings and I was in a great position to get a big fight in the US against fellow former world champion, Abner Mares. Just as the fight was close to being made, the world was hit by the COVID-19 pandemic in 2020 and what ensued took the whole world by storm.

Border closures meant any possibility of fighting in the US would now have to be put on hold. My team and I had to come up with another plan to stay active and keep my world ranking relevant. My home state of New South Wales was forced into a lockdown for the first time in March 2020 and it seemed like the whole world was put on pause. With gyms closed during this time, I stayed active by partaking in outdoor sessions with my boxing coach, Billy Hussein. I kept up my running and strength and conditioning sessions with Angelo. The idea was to stay in decent shape so we were ready to go whenever an opportunity presented itself. Just as was the case with the rest of the world, however, 2020 was largely written off by the pandemic.

Eventually, restrictions began to ease within NSW and Australia, with gyms allowed to open once again and events allowed back on. This meant we could get back into proper training and start planning our next move. We devised a plan to have me back in the ring on 30 January 2021; a whole thirteen months since my previous bout. The borders, however, were still closed. Our attempts at gaining an exemption to bring in a world-rated fighter from overseas were quashed and we were left with no choice but to bring in my next opponent, Joey Baylon, a highly credentialed former kickboxing world champion as a late replacement. Baylon, who was making his professional boxing debut, had amassed an impressive kickboxing record. The vision we had seen of him led us to believe he would provide a good challenge and would be able to give me some much-needed rounds, especially after the extensive time out of the ring. The vibes in the gym were high. My gym mates and I were just grateful to be back in that sort of environment. The camp, and lead-up to the fight, were smooth and I was ready to get back out and do what I do best: perform.

Baylon and I both made the agreed weight, and our battle was officially on. The energy in the venue that night was amazing, despite the restrictions on the number of people allowed. I was extremely buoyed by having Laith there with me at another fight. He was now a little older and already showing interest in boxing and throwing haymakers. I put in a solid performance, dropping Baylon in the second round before forcing the referee to stop the fight in the seventh, after dishing out some serious punishment. Baylon had proved a tough and awkward customer, using his experience in kickboxing to survive as long as he did, but ultimately it was another feather in my cap. Whilst I understood Baylon wasn't the sort of calibre of opponent we were hoping for, I was glad to be able to put the long layoff behind me and get another victory.

CHAPTER TWENTY-SIX
LAST FIGHT

My next bout didn't eventuate until nearly fourteen months after my victory over Baylon. After that fight, the COVID-19 pandemic was again wreaking havoc around the world and had put a halt on many boxing events taking place. I was forced to play the waiting game to work out what my next move would be, but eventually, my team were able to strike up a deal that would see me pitted against the world-rated and undefeated Lightweight, Jacob Ng. I had done some sparring with Ng a few years earlier, when his father brought him and a few others to Bodypunch Boxing Gym for some work. Ng was unusually tall for a lightweight but had always liked to fight and trade punches on the inside, ignoring his glaring height and reach advantages. He was considered one of Australia's most entertaining boxers at the time, but I felt it would make for a great match-up for me.

I was there to watch one of Ng's more recent bouts against the hard-hitting Hunter Ioane in a fight that was rated as Australian Boxing's 'Fight of the Year' for 2020. Ng was dropped hard in round one by a big right hand but did well to recover and stop his opponent a few rounds later in what was all-out war. Despite getting his hand raised that night, Ng showed he had many vulnerabilities, especially defensively. I had a feeling that night we would soon cross paths in the ring and pushed to make it happen. Just a week after that fight, I rang Ng's promoter, Angelo Di Carlo, to discuss making the fight happen. Di Carlo, who I had formed a great relationship with over the span of my boxing career, was adamant he wouldn't let the fight happen. He told me he had invested a lot of money in Jacob and was looking to get him a big fight opportunity. He obviously didn't want to take the risk of him in a fight with me, but he did say he'd consider making it happen if it made sense down the line.

Travel restrictions and quarantine rules meant it was pretty much impossible to bring international opponents to Australia. This meant many domestic match-ups between Australian fighters were being made and it began to work to our advantage. Billy Hussein would soon come to me with a proposition in making the fight against Ng. The deal entailed us coming up with a purse of AU$20,000 for Ng and putting the show on in Sydney. I quickly agreed, knowing we'd be able to come up with the money through ticket sales. The lure of making my way into the world ratings in the lightweight division was also enticing. I knew I had the tools to beat Ng, and doing so would put me firmly in the top five of the lightweight division in both the IBF and the WBO.

An agreement was made between both camps, but it wasn't long before we were met with a stumbling block. Growing COVID-19 case numbers led to tighter restrictions in NSW and a cap on the amount of people allowed in venues was reintroduced. This left us with little option but to have the fight staged in Ng's home state, Queensland, to be promoted by Angelo Di Carlo's ACE Boxing Promotions. The issue then became that I wouldn't be able to sell as many tickets in Queensland, making it harder to come up with Ng's agreed purse of $20,000. At this point, Sid stepped in as a benefactor and came up with the money. The terms were agreed upon by late September 2021, however the fight would need to be rescheduled several times until the date was finally set for 19 March 2022 in the Gold Coast. Despite the postponement and shuffling of dates, I stayed in the gym and on the running track to ready myself for battle.

The training camp in the lead-up to this fight was one of the hardest I'd gone through. Having had such a long time to prepare, we decided it would be best to break our camp down into segments. During the last part, I was forced to battle through injuries which threatened to derail the fight. The first real battle of the camp came in the form of plantar fasciitis in my right foot. I was sparring when it felt like someone had shot me in the bottom of the foot. I took a simple step, went to pivot and then immediately hit the deck, knowing something was seriously wrong with my foot. We immediately stopped sparring and I headed straight to my doctor to get it checked properly. The evidence pointed towards plantar fasciitis, so we needed to get to work to make sure I could get through the rigours of camp. I conscripted the help of a podiatrist who I checked in with every few days to help ease my pain. Dr Maher Said was instrumental in getting me through the remainder of the camp.

Just a few weeks out from the fight, during a body sparring session, I suffered some damage to my ribs. Whilst painful, I was able to manage it well enough and was able to put the finishing touches on a long and grinding training camp. I knew I was physically and mentally ready for anything Ng could throw at me on the night. For me, this was just another night in the office, but that definitely was not the case for him. I knew it was going to be the biggest stage he'd been on, whilst I had fought on some of the biggest stages there are and numerous big-time fights. I realised I had to use this to my advantage and call on my experience to tame this young lion.

The mental warfare truly began with a string of social media posts. I had played it cool in the entire lead-up to the fight, including the initial press conference which took place just over three weeks before the fight. As the fight edged closer, though, I wanted to get into Ng's head and began goading him with cheeky posts on social media. I knew I had an impact instantly, as he started to respond with his own posts. We traded barbs for a short time. It was all very much tongue-in-cheek, but I knew building it up this way would help me on fight night.

At the final press conference, I decided to take a few digs at Ng and his slender frame, reminding him of the struggle he would need to go through in order to make the lightweight limit. I even had someone from my team hand him an Uber Eats bag with empty pizza cartons. It was during the face-off that I knew I had truly gotten under his skin. 'I'm going to pick you up and dump you on your head,' he quipped. I knew I had him.

Come weigh-in day, I woke up 500g over the limit whilst being well-fed the night before. My weight cut didn't require too much work since I was a natural super featherweight moving up to lightweight, and the vibes in our camp were high. I was surrounded by my loved ones on the beautiful Gold Coast and it felt like something special was brewing. I completed my cut, jumped on my scales and was pleased to see that I was 61kg, meaning I had 200g to play with and still an hour or so until the commencement of the weigh-in.

The weigh-in, set to take place at The Star Gold Coast, had a Las Vegas feel about it. ACE Boxing Promotions went all-out in creating an amazing event and the buzz was electrifying. Ng and I were the first called to the scale. We both successfully made weight and faced off for the final time before meeting in the ring the following evening. With all of the pre-fight responsibilities out of the way, it was now time to refuel and get a good night's rest to perform at my best the next evening.

Finally, it was officially fight day! I was well-rested and ready to put on a great performance. I had put in so much work and gotten over quite a few hurdles to be in the ring that night and I was determined to enjoy it. In the back of my mind, I knew, win or lose, it could possibly be the last time I would be competing in a boxing ring. I was solely fixated, however, on a big victory and wasn't about to let all the hard work during camp go to waste. I told myself that with a sharp mind and intense focus for the full ten rounds, there was no way in the world that Ng could beat me.

It was soon time to head down to the venue and enter the dressing rooms, flanked by a few of my loved ones. I had aimed to stay as relaxed and comfortable as possible in the lead-up to the bout itself. I had some music playing in the room as I got my hands wrapped by my long-serving cornerman, Brian Wilmott. Brian is legendary within the Australian boxing circle and his experience comes to the fore during these times. He is a master at wrapping hands and keeping a fighter relaxed, with his light-hearted conversation and constant positive talk. It's invaluable at a time that can be the most nerve-wracking, as you sit there thinking about all work you've put in and what would happen once the first bell rang.

With my hands wrapped, it was time to loosen up, get limber and get in the zone. Having Laith in the dressing room, chasing me around and trying to land a blow gave me a massive boost and kept me smiling the entire time. It's a memory I will cherish forever. We got my fight gloves on and my trainer, Billy Hussein, and I began going over all we had worked on during camp. I pounded the pads with speed and precision, feeling sharp as I did so. That is always a confidence booster before a fight. I was ready to lay it all out in the ring.

The entrance music I chose was specifically to keep me loose and relaxed as I danced my way out to the ring. I promised my good friend Adam Houda I'd come out to 'Ain't Nobody' by Chaka Khan and that I'd enjoy the moment, not allowing myself to tighten up. The crowd was raucous and I was having the time of my life as I busted out the dance moves, vibing to an all-time classic song. Jacob Ng was known for his lavish ring entrances, but I really felt I had bested him on that front too.

When Ng entered the ring, I stepped to him and got in his face to let him know I was right there and ready to get into it. I took a glance down and realised there was a rip in the gloves he had on. I pointed it out to Billy Hussein and he was quick to inform the referee about the rip. After taking a look at it, the referee decided that the gloves were not fit for competition and ordered a different set of gloves to be given to Ng. After a short delay, the ring announcer began with the introductions, and we were soon centre ring listening to the referee's instructions before the first bell. We touched gloves, I headed back to my corner and gave Billy H a hug, reading the Fatiha as I always do before fights. Ding! Ding! The first bell rings.

The first round went very much as we expected. We had planned and were prepared for Ng coming out fast. Ng tries to swarm his opponents with his high work rate and in-your-face style, so the idea was to frustrate him early with evasive foot movement and intelligent in-fighting. I wanted to prove that Ng's height, reach and overall size advantage was not going to be a major factor in the fight and had to prove so early. When we were on the inside, I held my ground and would not allow him to push me back. A major part of our game plan was to not let him have any of the ascendency, as he is a fighter who feeds off confidence. He knew very early on that he was in a 'proper' fight.

The next few rounds went back and forth as we both landed decent shots in some exciting exchanges, but I could feel him slowing down as the rounds ticked over. By the end of the fourth round, his legs were appearing a lot wearier, and I began to feel he was not as strong in the clinch as he had been earlier. My corner reiterated how tired he was looking and the message was clear. It was time to pour some pressure on. I came out for the fifth round with a spring in my step and was determined to push Ng back and land some telling blows. I had my best round and the tide had completely turned in my favour.

Coming back to the corner after the fifth round, Billy and Hussy were imploring me to stay in his face and on his chest, telling me I was safer on the inside and was winning more of the exchanges now. The bell rang for the sixth and I came out on the front foot behind some head movement. Less than fifteen seconds into the round during an exchange, Ng found his way under my right shoulder. I rested my arm over his neck for what felt like a second or two, and before I knew it, I had been flipped on to my back, landing directly on my rib cage. Immediately, I was out of breath and in excruciating pain and was staring up at the ceiling when I could feel the referee's leg next to me. I grabbed his leg and begged him to help me. The ringside doctor was rushed into the ring and it was clear I was in no state to continue. I was helped up onto a stool as I was announced the winner via disqualification in the sixth round. The referee and commission correctly deeming Ng's hip-toss style throw an illegal move, and since I couldn't continue, I was ruled the winner.

It was not the way I had wanted to win and put a big dampener on what was turning out to be a great fight and great event in general.

I was helped into my change room, and the ringside doctor diagnosed I had some ribs out of place or possibly fractured. An ambulance was called and I was taken to Gold Coast Hospital where it was confirmed I had suffered a dislodged rib and three separate fractures in the area. I was kept overnight in hospital and had a long road to recovery. I was extremely upset that I didn't get the chance to win the fight the way I should have and was now going to need to be in a sling for the foreseeable future.

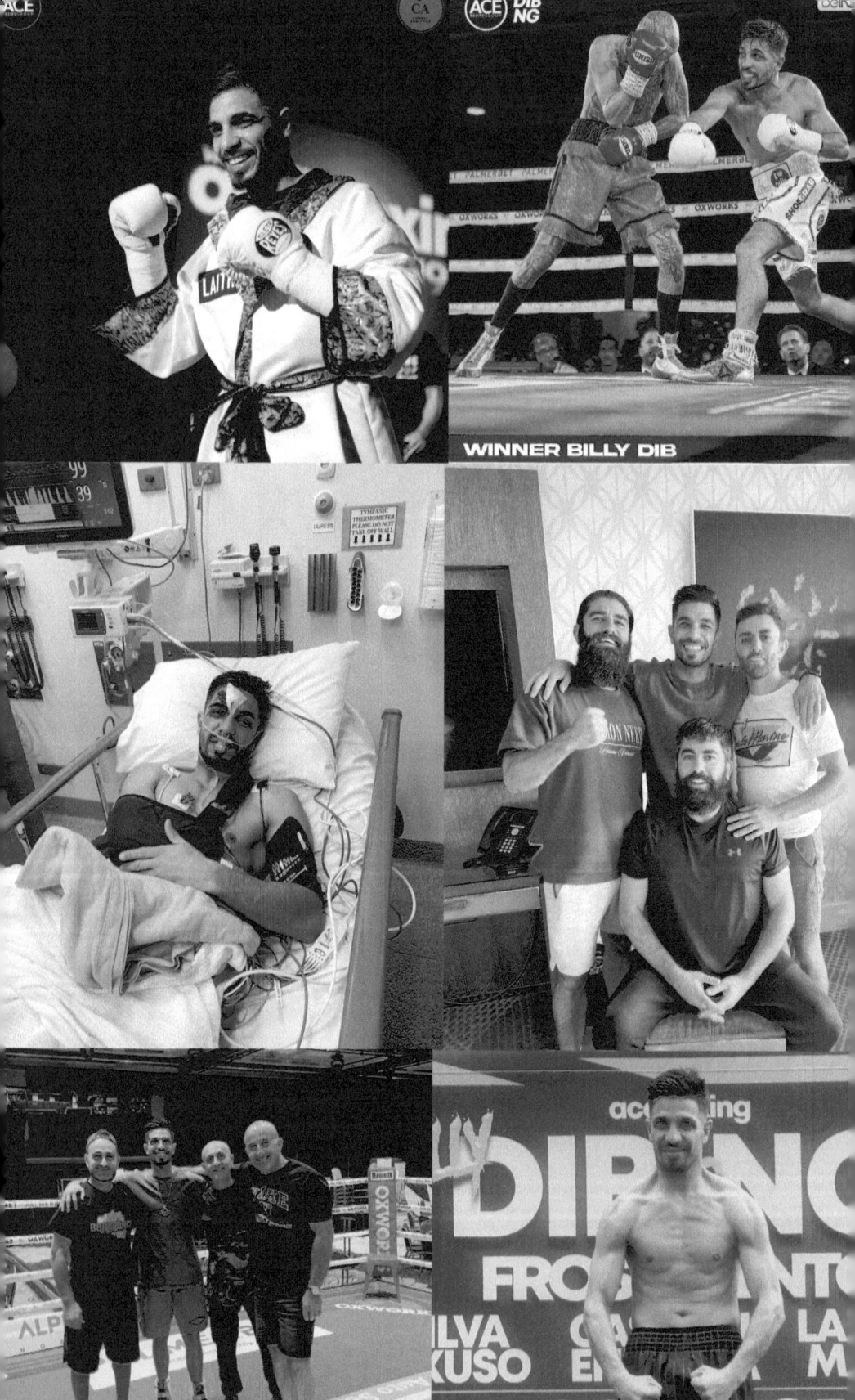

CHAPTER TWENTY-SEVEN
MY JOURNEY THROUGH CANCER

Day in, day out, I was dealing with a sharp pain to the right side of my lower abdomen. Feeling sick on a daily basis, I quickly lost my appetite. After multiple days of pain, I took the advice of my Uncle Angelo and called the medical centre. On 13 October 2022, I contacted Faisal Rifi notifying him of the intolerable pain I'd been dealing with. He told me to head to the medical centre in Belmore and he would take me directly in to see Dr Vani. As promised by Faisal, I arrived at the doctors and was attended to immediately. To ease the pain, I was given Panadol and a blood test was taken, as well as a urine sample. Dr Vani asked me several questions about my bowel movements, appetite and so on, before coming to the conclusion that a CT scan was necessary. I left Belmore Medical Centre and headed to Campsie to get the CT scan. I was given a litre of water when I arrived, and shortly after, was taken in for the scan. They said they would send me results later in the day.

On my way home, I stopped back at Belmore Medical to pick up what I needed to test my faeces, as the doctor also wanted to send that off for testing.

For a few days the pain lingered, but it was bearable. That was until Thursday 20 October 2022. I headed to the gym for my usual 9:30am boxing session, and as well as to meet Brian, my cutman. During the session, I began to feel abnormally sharp pains. Billy Hussein told me to rest up as I didn't look myself.

I packed my bag and headed off to Riverwood to get some breakfast with Brian. It had been days since I'd eaten properly, so I decided on a detox juice and acai bowl. Brian and I chatted away, but my pain was in overdrive; the green juice I had was causing me serious pain. I had a few spoons of the acai bowl which made things even worse. I tried to stay calm and focus on the positives as Brian and I chatted. When we said our goodbyes, I raced home, as I felt my bladder was going to explode.

Moments later, I contacted my wife, Berry, letting her know I was in excruciating pain and was about to call an ambulance.

Berry became very distressed, but I assured her it would be okay for her to carry on with her day, as she had taken Laith to a swimming class.

I then contacted 000 and told them of my pain. They arrived after twenty minutes and took some notes before walking me to the ambulance parked in front of my home. The medic passed me a green whistle and I began to inhale it. It made me light-headed but didn't do much for the pain. On arriving at Canterbury Hospital, everything seemed to be flowing until the medics asked me to sit on a chair and wait for a nurse to take a COVID-19 test. Frustrated and in agonising pain, doctors walked by me as I pleaded for help.

It was in that moment I had a brain explosion and smashed one of the hospital monitors onto the floor! Suddenly, I had the hospital's attention. They finally saw the pain I was dealing with. I was taken to a room with a bed and given an injection of morphine; the sensation of what was injected made me feel so strange. An hour later, I was deemed COVID-free and wheeled into the emergency section where I again gave a urine and blood sample for testing.

After six hours, I was told nothing was detected in my samples and I should book in with a specialist for an endoscopy. I was given my discharge papers. Confused and high on morphine, I contacted my brother Youssef asking him to pick me up from Bankstown Hospital (remember: I was actually at Canterbury Hospital). Close to thirty minutes passed when I contacted Youssef again. He told me he was outside waiting for me. It was only when I made my way outside, I realised my mistake. I notified my brother and booked an Ola to take me home. When I arrived, I laid down in an effort to gather myself. Berry had scheduled a meeting with her friend, Fida, so I took Laith and headed to my parents' house. Mum offered to make me tea and I accepted; the first thing I'd eaten since trying to eat breakfast earlier in the day. At that stage, I wasn't feeling any pain, until I decided to have some Lebanese bread. The pain kicked in again – on overdrive. I began to wonder if perhaps I could have coeliac disease. I tried my best to keep my mind off the pain by watching an old movie classic, *The Combination*, which featured a friend of mine, Firass Dirani.

By this point, Berry had arrived and was sharing a conversation with my sister, Sabrina, as I continued to try and hide my pain. At around 11pm Berry, Laith and I headed home.

My mind was not prepared for what I would face during the night. I tossed and turned from the pain, waiting for 5am to finally come. It was Fajr time. I performed my Wudu and morning prayer. I asked the Almighty Allah to ease my pain. As I sat on the couch, Berry woke up and attended to me. She made me a 'hot pack' and headed back upstairs. I took two Panadeine Forte before following her up, and they absolutely knocked me out. It was now the morning of 21 October 2022 – Friday, the Holy Day was upon us. I woke at around 11am, still in excruciating pain, and asked Berry to drop me at my parents' house so I could collect my car and head to Friday prayers.

It was on the way there that Nancy, from Dr Rifi's office, contacted me to say I would not be able to see a specialist for an endoscopy until Monday. I became infuriated. I contacted the specialist myself who confirmed they would not be able to fit me in until Monday morning.

'Ma'am,' I said, 'by Monday morning I'll likely be dead from this pain.'

Her response was blunt. 'Sir, if you are in so much pain, don't call us, contact 000 and head to the emergency ward.' She was right, but all I could think about was my horrible experience at Canterbury Hospital the previous day. When I arrived at my parents' place, I was greeted at the door by my mother who could see the agonising pain I was in. She suggested I may have caught a bug! I once again became very frustrated as I felt no-one was understanding what I was going through.

As I lay on the floor of their lounge room, I pleaded with my sister, Sabrina, to call an ambulance. I felt like I was dying. She rang 000 and notified them of my excruciating pain. The first thing they asked was, 'Is the man vaccinated? Is everyone in the home vaccinated?' She was then told that when the ambulance arrived, 'Everyone was to wear a mask.'

I became so angry, I told my sister to, 'Hang up on that bitch.'

The previous day at the hospital I had been given a prescription for some medication. I asked my brother, Youssef, to collect it so I could see if it would help with the pain.

It was in that moment my brother, Mohammed, rang asking me how I was. I explained the excruciating pain I was experiencing and how no-one believed what I was dealing with. He then called a close friend of his by the name of Dr Pran, who contacted me and suggested I go to Norwest Private Hospital in Bella Vista. He told me he would notify his friends I was coming and everything would be taken care of.

My brother Youssef then drove me to Bella Vista to drop me at emergency. I told him to go home and I would contact him to let them know what was happening. With the pain I was experiencing, I really didn't think I'd be going home any time soon. When I walked into the emergency ward, I thought the receptionist would know who I was when I mentioned my name, as Dr Pran had told me he would notify them I was coming. What I failed to do was to mention Dr Pran. I was given several forms to fill out and sent to the waiting room. I couldn't believe I was going to be sitting, waiting, in an emergency room once again, in excruciating pain. The next thirty minutes were absolute hell. When I couldn't deal with the pain anymore, I headed outside as I was feeling terribly sick, and proceeded to vomit.

Minutes later, I woke up on the floor of the hospital with a man slapping my face.

'Sir! Sir. Wake up.'

I looked up at the man and said, 'I think I'm dying.'

'No, mate – you have a pulse.'

The next thing I remember was waking up in the emergency ward with Dr Sanjay sat by my hospital bed, asking me to explain what I was experiencing. He was a little confused when I asked him if he thought it might be cancer and he replied, 'No, I don't think so.' He suggested I might have stomach ulcers or inflammation in my bowels. Nevertheless, he would get to the bottom of it by doing another CT scan, as well as an ultrasound in the morning.

The following morning, I was collected from my room and taken for the ultrasound. The nurse was thorough, looking at every single spot on my abdomen – except for where the pain was. I showed her exactly where it was, and bingo, she found something. She contacted Dr Bahin, notifying him of her findings. He told her to prepare me for a CT scan so they could investigate further what was happening. After a few hours, Dr Bahin woke me to say they had located something, but he wasn't sure what it was. He would need to do an endoscopy to confirm it. I had to drink a special liquid to empty my bowels, so he was able to see clearly what he was looking at. Around 7pm that night, I was taken for the endoscopy, and that's when my life flashed before my eyes. Dr Bahin woke me up after my minor operation to tell me what I had thought for the past few days.

'Billy, I have located the source of your pain. Would you like the good news or the bad news first?'

'What's the good news, doctor?' I said.

'Billy, the good news is we don't often perform surgeries on Sundays, but we are going to operate on you tomorrow. Now for the bad news. We have located a cancerous tumour in your colon. I'm not sure what stage it's at, but we need to remove it – urgently.' He then asked if I could contact one of my family members and let him speak to them. I suggested he speak to my wife, Berry, and my older brother, Jihad, and let them know what was happening.

Not in a very good state, as I was only just waking up from the anaesthetic, I called Berry. She answered the phone asking how I was and how I was feeling. I told her they had found cancer in my colon. She was in shock, distressed and crying. Dr Bahin calmed her down and connected Jihad to the call. He was calling them to let them know I was going into surgery to remove the cancer.

The following morning, my good friend Atal visited me and accompanied me to the theatre room. Dr Sanjay would be performing the procedure. As he spoke of the operation that was set to take place, I couldn't stop myself from shaking. He told me he had a 97% strike rate and had performed the same operation, successfully, many times in the past. I signed a disclaimer accepting there was a chance things could go wrong. I said a prayer and put my trust and faith in the Almighty Allah. Atal stayed with me until I was entering the theatre room. He gave me a hug and said, 'See you soon.'

I was so nervous. What happened next, I haven't a clue. The anaesthetist asked me a question and when I woke up, I was in a room surrounded by family, relatives and friends. If it wasn't for my cousins recording and showing me, I'd have no clue what was going on. My body was so very tired and back-to-back operations had left me in so much pain.

It was another seven days in hospital before I was allowed home and then I spent three or four days at my parents' house. I was under strict instructions not to strain my body, and when I first left hospital, I was unable to manage the stairs in my own home, so Mum and Dad's it was. They were super cautious and took great care of me, feeding me much better food than I had in hospital! I have to add at this point that despite my condition, I was a little shocked at the food I was served in hospital; hot food on plastic plates and hot drinks in plastic cups. I believe the quality of food we fuel our bodies with is so important for overall health. I believe in eating good-quality fresh food for good nutrition and I am surprised this is not a priority in everyone's treatment. But I guess that's a story for another day!

The doctors didn't give me much advice, except to say I couldn't do any boxing training for at least six months. My first thought was that they didn't know me or my mindset, and that I'd be back training within a month! My next appointment date was scheduled for Monday

7 November, where we were to discuss further treatment. I was very much against chemotherapy. In my mind, they had removed the cancer and I would soon be ready to get back in the gym.

But I didn't make it to my next scheduled appointment. Friday 4 November was a day and night I will never forget. It was Friday morning. I contacted Atal to meet at Levant prior to heading to Friday prayers.

I started my morning taking some black seed oil and honey as the Prophet Muhammad SWS said black seed would cure everything besides death. I then made my way to meet Atal at Levant for some breakfast. I had eggs, mushrooms and spinach as well as some tea.

Shortly after, we headed to prayers before returning to Levante for a light lunch. After leaving, I started to feel unwell and my stomach was a little sore. I met Berry at home before we left to visit her mum. During our visit, I began to feel some serious pain in my stomach. Berry's mum had cooked some rice and chicken, so I decided to have a light bite. What a mistake that was! The pain kicked in on overdrive – again. I decided to take a hot bath which did nothing to ease the pain.

Berry and I had made plans to meet up with her relatives. When we arrived at Rabia's home, I had trouble walking to her front door, I was in excruciating pain. I took a seat before asking Berry's cousin, Bilal, if he could give me some painkillers. They suggested I eat some fruit before taking some Nurofen, which did very little to combat the pain. I couldn't handle the pain anymore, so got up to try and walk it off. Berry was in the front room praying and once she finished her prayers, I asked her if I could lay down on the bed as I couldn't handle the pain anymore. Moments later, the pain became intolerable. Berry called her cousin Bilal to look over me, and everyone pleaded with me to go to the hospital.

Berry called Dr Sanjay who instructed her to get me directly to the hospital. Bilal and his brother, Shereef, escorted me to the car and we made our way back to Norwest Private Hospital. What a night I was in for! To say I saw death would be an understatement. Arriving at the hospital, I was on struggle street, not knowing what was wrong. The doctors tried to ease my pain by giving me morphine, while I tried to remain calm as Berry and my son, Laith, sat at my bedside.

Once things seemed under control, Berry and my son left the hospital. Moments later, I began to vomit profusely. The pain continued until around 5am and I must have vomited close to thirty times. I had never experienced physical pain like it in my whole life, even though I'd been battered and bruised a few times in the ring. At one point I was asking the Almighty to take away the pain or take me! Allah (SWT) tells us, 'If my servant asks, I will deliver,' and in that moment, a big and strong Afghan nurse,came to my rescue.

'Help me,' I pleaded.

His response was, 'I will help you … but you need to help me to help you.' He explained he needed me to swallow a tube that would be inserted through my nose, down my throat and into my stomach. He warned it would not be easy, but if I trusted him, I would stop vomiting. I had asked Allah to help me stop vomiting and help had arrived. One nurse held my hand for support, another held a cup near my mouth. The head nurse began to insert the tube, and as painful as it was to swallow, I simply couldn't stand to vomit one more time. Minutes, later the ordeal was over, and as promised by this amazing nurse, the vomiting stopped.

Hours later, I woke feeling drugged and drowsy. I could see a familiar face although I couldn't talk. It was Atal – what a beautiful and supportive man he has been since I met him. Atal stayed with me for hours, even though I was unable to speak or entertain him. Later that day, I was taken to my own room to rest and recover. A few hours on,

Berry turned up with Laith, my mum, Lina and Fida. The tube that was in my nose was really starting to agitate me so I asked Berry to contact Dr Sanjay to see if it could be removed. Having it removed was such a relief; finally, I felt normal again.

In the evening, I was visited by Dr Abir, a haematologist, who would be taking over my treatment. Dr Abir explained the pain was caused because the lymph nodes in my stomach were inflamed and causing a blockage. He explained the results from my blood tests had come in and what they thought was colon cancer was, in fact, Burkit lymphoma cancer. It's a cancer the attacks the lymphs and is a fast spreader. In that moment, everything froze for me. I began to cry as I looked at my mum. All I could think about was how I didn't want to leave my wife and son. How could this be? I just wanted to go home and wake up from this nightmare. After shedding some tears, I dusted myself off and put my trust and faith in Allah, accepting his decree for me. The first step to healing is surrendering to the Almighty decree. This is what he had ordained for me and all I could do was to accept it and be strong. Alhamdulillah for everything.

The next step was to get a PET scan to work out how much the cancer had spread, as we have thousands of lymph nodes in our bodies. The next day, in the morning, I was transported to a clinic to get the PET scan. I was being looked after by a gentleman by the name of Larry; what a man he was. He comforted me and assured me, 'You'll get through this.' Moments after meeting him, he said to me, 'You look very familiar.'

I responded by telling him my name was Billy Dib and I was a former World Champion. He snapped his fingers and said, 'I knew it. Come on, brother, let's get this done.'

After prepping me, it was time for the scan. I laid down as the liquid was administered. I prayed to God the whole time, begging him to not let me light up like a Christmas tree. At some point, I fell into what seemed like a deep sleep, and what I saw was the Lakemba Maghsal – the place where we wash the dead.

I was being washed by my brothers Jihad, Emaid, Mohammed, Nasser, Youssef and Angelo. I was confused. I woke up from this dream with Larry telling me we were done.

I asked, 'Larry, be honest, did I light up like a Christmas tree?'

'No, my friend,' he said, 'hand on heart, you hardly lit up at all.'

Thank you, God, once again you have answered my prayers. Still waking up, the first call I received was from Angelo. 'Ang, my brother, are you a Muslim?' I asked him.

His response was, 'Bill – if you want me to be Muslim, I'll do that for you.'

I told Angelo of my dream and how it was a sign.

The same day, Dr Abir visited me at Norwest and told me I would be transported to Westmead Public Hospital for my treatment that night.

CHAPTER TWENTY-EIGHT
THE ROLLER-COASTER CALLED CANCER

- **The Prayers** – It's what keeps everything in perspective; knowing what I am going through is part of God's plan for me, to grow stronger and more resilient and be the best dad I can be for my son.
- **The Crying** – Never did I expect to release so much emotion for myself. I went through a lot of crying at Sara's passing, of course, but this time, I've been more aware of it. The crying never stops. And it's not just me, but my close friends and family too.
- **The Vomiting** – mmm … do we really need to go there? Let's just say I was NOT prepared for the level of vomiting I would experience through my cancer journey!
- **The Anxiety** – Anxiety is what is experienced when you worry about the future. Obviously, it's a big issue when your life is hanging in the balance and you have a beautiful wife and son you want

to grow old with. Anxiety is a crippling affliction as part of the cancer journey.

- **My Mum** – My rock. A gem of a human being. When I was in hospital, fighting for my life, I begged her to go home and rest, but she wouldn't listen to me! She stayed with me, every day. Every time I woke, she was there on her knees, praying for God's protection.
- **My Siblings: The Roster** – The whole family came together to make sure I made it through the really tough times during my treatment. My five brothers and sister Sabrina made a roster to ensure someone was with me every day. I actually felt bad for them. There were times I was so sick and in and out of consciousness, I would tell them to go home, that I didn't want them there. But they stuck with me – every day – and I am so grateful for their support and love.
- **An Inspirational Visitor** – On the morning of 15 November, I was graced with a visit from a wonderful and inspirational friend. Ismail in Musa Menk is a Zimbabwean Islamic scholar, known as Mufti Menk. He is the Grand Mufti of Zimbabwe's muslim community, which makes up roughly 1% of the country's population. He is the head of the fatwa department of the Council of Islamic Scholars in Zimbabwe. His visit was so uplifting. He assured me he had a good feeling that I would overcome the cancer and my future was bright. It gave me renewed hope and reassurance, as I know Mufti Menk is a man of God. I really appreciated his visit.
- **The Treatment** – The discovery, pain and acknowledgement of cancer, along with the necessary operations, is such a small part of the cancer journey. It's the treatment that's all-encompassing and during the treatment, when my life was on a knife's edge, I could have given up so many times. I literally saw death on many occasions and if it wasn't for God's mercy, I'd never have made it

through. Because of the disease I have, I had to stay as an in-patient in the public hospital system, despite having full private health cover. The public hospital was the only place I could receive the treatment I required. I had a total of seven weeks in hospital – the first stay was twenty-eight days. I had times when I would be on an infusion of Methotrexate for twenty-three hours straight, which caused ulcers in my throat, immense pain and persistent vomiting. Which leads me to ...

- **The Nurses** – A huge thanks must be acknowledged for the wonderful nurses who have assisted me during my treatment. They have all been amazing! One nurse, in particular, gave me the inspiration to fight on. She told me to fight hard for my son. Every time I felt down or I felt I was near the end, she reminded me that I needed to survive – for Laith.
- **The Healing Process** – I am so thankful, and it's been very therapeutic, to have Sid David, my life coach and mentor, available to 'listen' when I need to talk. He never interrupts but says all the right things at exactly the right time. He's been a true godsend. But the greatest medicine I've had is family and friends. Each time I come home from hospital, my son, wife and family give me the strength I need to continue to fight. Life is so precious – I never want to leave my son. This sickness has taught me so much about showing your loved ones just how much you care – every single day. In some cases (like in a car accident, or sudden heart attack), you don't have the opportunity to say goodbye, so show and tell them how much they mean to you. Now more than ever, my highest priority is to share love and laughter with the people who matter most in my life.

ENDORSEMENT
MONIQUE MAYERS

My most cherished and memorable moment working with Billy Dib was in Macau, China, for the Dib vs. Gradovich rematch on HBO. I was the chief operating officer for his then promotion company and along with my colleague, Angel Martinez, handled every aspect of the company's business.

While in China, Billy asked that I accompany him and his team during his ring walk. I was more than honoured to do so for multiple reasons. Not only was Billy dedicated to the sport of boxing, but the love, respect and dedication towards his family was beyond admirable and to be included with his team/family at that very moment was a humbling, heartfelt experience for me.

Although we did not get the win in China, I believe there is no dishonour in losing a fight. There's only dishonour in not fighting because you are afraid to lose, and Billy gave 100% that night. The fans in attendance were proof of just that. Despite his loss, while walking through the Venetian hotel that same evening, a sea of fans surrounded Billy and in unison began chanting his name ... 'Billy, Billy!' That was a true display and testament to his character.

Billy persevered through what one may deem as a tumultuous professional career and even greater loss personally with the passing of his first wife, yet is the TRUE champion through it all. He never compromised his dignity, integrity and morals despite challenging times and I will forever respect him for that.

Billy and his team were nothing short of professional, honest and respectful.

I believe God makes no mistakes, and I am truly blessed to have been a part of Billy's journey.

Monique Mayers

ENDORSEMENT
MRS CHETTY

Billy's journey to success has sent a clear and indelible message to the world. 'Strive to do your best. Never fear to dream big.' The proverb by Ben Franklin, 'Nothing ventured, nothing gained,' truly personifies what Billy represents.

In 1995, Billy started Heathcote High School as a year seven student. I was his English teacher and Billy approached me at the end of the lesson stating that he needed help to consolidate his reading skills. I offered Billy individual lunchtime lessons which he readily agreed to participate in. He never missed a lesson, which was rather rare for a year seven student. In Billy I recognised determination, motivation and diligence. His sacrifice, coupled with his humility, paid off as his literacy skills improved substantially.

During our chats, Billy always expressed his love for boxing and repeatedly told me that that one day he would become a famous boxer as that was his ambition in life. I particularly have vivid memories of Billy in my year ten English class. He always carried a gym bag, together with his school bag and would conscientiously complete his tasks so that he would be ready to leave on the bell to attend his training sessions.

I can still remember our conversations when Billy would tell me that he was going to become a world-famous boxer one day. I tried my utmost to discourage Billy, telling him that he had to be realistic, but he was adamant. In retrospect, I was not intentionally trying to burst his bubble, but rather spare him future disappointments as students often mention that they would like to become famous in their future pursuits.

But Billy had other plans. This youngster had 'fire in his belly' and would not change his plans. I am so glad that he did not heed my advice. Instead, I have shared memorable moments with my family cheering Billy on when his fights were televised. I have to say that I am so incredibly proud of this self-made man, Billy Bib.

Your enthusiasm, determination and diligence should serve as a shining beacon and an inspiration to the rest of the world. You have reached for the stars and you shone with them.

Congratulations and good luck.
Much love,
Mrs Sharla Chetty.

My beloved father and mother. Two humans who I owe my life to.